COLLI

Cycling
in
CUMBRIA
& THE LAKE DISTRICT

HarperCollins*Publishers*

Published by Collins
An imprint of HarperCollins*Publishers*
77-85 Fulham Palace Road
London W6 8JB

First published 1998
Text © HarperCollins*Publishers* 1998
Maps © Bartholomew 1998

Routes compiled by Mike Hutchinson and Neil Wheadon.
Design by Creative Matters Design Consultancy, Glasgow.
Typeset by Bob Vickers.

Photographs reproduced by kind permission of the following:
Cumbria Tourist Board pages 53, 61, 62; V.K. Guy pages 35, 69, 111;
International Photobank pages 29, 42; Bill Meadows pages 11, 15, 22,
24, 31, 41, 44-5, 47, 49, 50, 81, 93, 107; National Trust page 33;
Simon Warner pages 19, 64-5, 70, 101, 105; Neil Wheadon pages 77, 89;
Andy Williams pages 5, 8, 37, 39, 57, 58, 72-3, 75, 85.

The landscape is changing all the time. While every care has
been taken in the preparation of this guide, the Publisher accepts
no responsibility whatsoever for any loss, damage, injury or
inconvenience sustained or caused as a result of using this guide.

Printed in Italy

ISBN 0 00 448683 8
98/1/14

CONTENTS

KEY TO ROUTES

Route colour coding

undemanding rides compiled specifically with families in mind
15-25km (10-15 miles)

middle distance rides suitable for all cyclists
25-40km (15-25 miles)

half-day rides for the more experienced and adventurous cyclist
40-60km (25-40 miles)

challenging full-day rides
over 60km (over 40 miles)

grande randonnée – a grand cycling tour
100km (60 miles)

 Routes marked with this symbol are off-road or have off-road sections
(includes well-surfaced cycleways as well as rougher off-road tracks)

Ullswater

LOCATION MAP

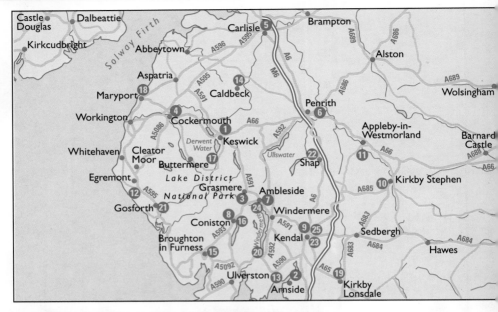

KEY TO ROUTE MAPS

M23	Motorway	
A259	'A' road / Dual carriageway	
B2130	'B' road / Dual carriageway	
	Good minor road	
	Minor road	
	Track / bridleway	
	Railway / station	
	Canal / river	
	Lake	
50	Contour (height in metres)	

	Cycle route
	Optional route
	Start of cycle route
12	Route direction
B	Place of interest
	Public house
	Café / refreshments
X	Restaurant
	Convenience store
P	Parking

☎	Telephone
☲	Picnic site
▲	Camping site
⚦	Public toilets
†	Place of worship
⚘	Viewpoint
⚑	Golf course
⁎	Tumulus
	Urban area
	Woodland

Height above sea level

50	100	150	200	300	400	500	600	700	800	900 metres
165	330	490	655	985	1315	1645	1975	2305	2635	2965 feet

INTRODUCTION

How to use this guide

Collins' *Cycling in Cumbria and the Lake District* has been devised for those who want trips out on their bicycles along quiet roads and tracks, passing interesting places and convenient refreshment stops without having to devise their own routes. Each of the 25 routes in this book has been compiled and ridden by an experienced cyclist for cyclists of all abilities.

Cycling in Cumbria and the Lake District is easy to use. Routes range from undemanding rides compiled specifically with families in mind to challenging full-day rides; the type of route is easily identified by colour coding (see page 5). At the start of each route an information box summarises: total distance (in kilometres/miles - distances have been rounded up or down throughout to the nearest 0.5km/mile and are approximate only); grade (easy, moderate or strenuous based on distance and difficulty); terrain; an average time to allow for the route; directions to the start of the route by car and, if appropriate, by train.

Each route is fully mapped and has concise, easy-to-follow directions. Comprehensive information on places of interest and convenient refreshment stops along each route are also given. Accumulated mileages within each route description give an indication of progress, while the profile diagram is a graphic representation of gradients along the route. These should be used as a guide only.

The following abbreviations are used in the route directions:

LHF	left hand fork
RHF	right hand fork
SO	straight on
SP	signpost
TJ	T junction
TL	turn left
TR	turn right
XR	crossroads

Cycling in Cumbria and the Lake District

Cumbria and the Lake District were already attracting great numbers of tourists before Wordsworth wrote his famous *Guide to the Lakes* in the last half of the 19th century. Today the wild beauty of the mountains, lakes and fells, traditional countryside, the coastline and seaside resorts attract thousands of visitors. There are ancient stone circles, roman remains, medieval castles, museums and, of course, attractions dedicated to Cumbria's famous writers such as William Wordsworth and Beatrix Potter – all of which are covered by the rides in this book.

The rides are intended to stay away from busy main roads as much as possible, following lanes, bridleways and single track roads. However, because of the nature of the landscape, there is a scarcity of roads in some areas, and short stretches of main roads have had to be included.

The soaring fells, mountain passes and valleys also mean that few of the rides escape hilly sections. However, the marvellous views will more than compensate for the effort of uphill cycling, and a hard uphill section usually means a following downhill swoop (you can always walk your bike up the steeper inclines).

The Cumbria Cycle Way is a 450km (280 mile) circular route around Cumbria. It links with the West Cumbria Cycle Network, which runs north to south along the west coast of Cumbria. For further information contact Cumbria County Council on (01228) 606336.

Geology, geography and history

The dramatic Cumbrian landscape is formed from three major rock bands. To the north and west are the rounded hills of the Skiddaw Slates, amongst the oldest rocks in the world, formed from sediment laid down some 530 million years ago. The central Lake District, roughly northeast to southwest, is composed of the the high craggy fells of the Borrowdale Volcanics, created through volcanic action. The gentle round hills of Silurian Rock, to the south, were formed between 440 and 410 million years ago, from layers of calcareous material, grit and mud, and provides the distinctive green slate often used in building Limestone and sandstone fringe the area, and there are pockets of granite, such as that at Shap. The Ice Age, around one and a half million years ago, hollowed out valleys and lake beds leaving the landscape seen today.

There is evidence of primitive Stone Age occupation, remains of Bronze and Iron Age settlements, and, of course, Roman occupation Norsemen settled the area, coming down from

Derwent Water

the west coast of Scotland. Much of Cumbrian history, though, evolved through the border conflicts between Scotland and England – Cumberland was Scottish for large periods of time. The legacy of the conflicts can be seen in the numerous castles and fortified houses.

The Lake District National Park was created in 1951 to protect the landscape from unsuitable development, allow public access and meet the needs of those who live and work in the area. It covers 2292 square km (885 square miles) and is the largest National Park in England and Wales. The National Park Authority exercises planning control, provides information and park rangers, and maintains footpaths and bridleways. It has a Visitor Centre at Brockhole, on the shore of Lake Windermere (see Route 7). The National Trust is the largest landowner in the Lake District, owning nearly a quarter of the land within the Park boundary. The National Park Authority and the National Trust, together with the Forestry Commission, Water Authorities and other landowners, provide protected public access over a huge area, unrivalled anywhere else in Britain. Cumbria and the Lake District is, as Wordsworth said, 'a sort of national property', for those 'with eyes to perceive and hearts to enjoy'.

Preparing for a cycling trip

Basic maintenance

A cycle ride is an immense pleasure, particularly on a warm sunny day. Nothing is better than coasting along a country lane gazing over the countryside. Unfortunately, not every cycling day is as perfect as this, and it is important to make sure that your bike is in good order and that you are taking the necessary clothing and supplies with you.

Before you go out on your bicycle check that everything is in order. Pump the tyres up if needed, and check that the brakes are working properly and that nothing is loose – the brakes are the only means of stopping quickly and safely. If there is a problem and you are not sure that you can fix it, take the bike to a cycle repair shop – they can often deal with small repairs very quickly.

When you go out cycling it is important to take either a puncture repair kit or a spare inner tube – it is often quicker to replace the inner tube in the event of a puncture, though it may be a good idea to practise first. You also need a pump, and with a slow puncture the pump may be enough to get you home. To remove the tyre you need a set of tyre levers. Other basic tools are an Allen key and a spanner. Some wheels on modern bikes can be removed by quick release levers built into the bike. Take a lock for your bike and if you have to leave it at any time, leave it in public view and locked through the frame and front wheel to something secure.

What to wear and take with you

It is not necessary to buy specialised cycling clothes. If it is not warm enough to wear shorts wear trousers which are easy to move in but fairly close to the leg below the knee – leggings are ideal – as this stops the trousers catching the chain. If you haven't got narrow-legged trousers, bicycle clips will hold them in. Jeans are not a good idea as they are rather tight and difficult to cycle in, and if they get wet they take a long time to dry. If your shorts or trousers are thin you might get a bit sore from being too long on the saddle. This problem can be reduced by using a gel saddle, and by wearing thicker, or extra, pants. Once you are a committed cyclist you can buy cycling shorts; or undershorts which have a protective pad built in and which can be worn under anything. It is a good idea to wear several thin layers of clothes so that you can add or remove layers as necessary. A zip-fronted top gives easy temperature control. Make sure you have something warm and something waterproof.

If you wear shoes with a firm, flat sole you will be able to exert pressure on the pedals easily, and will have less work to do to make the bicycle move. Gloves not only keep your hands warm but protect them in the event that you come off, and cycling mittens which cushion your hands are not expensive. A helmet is not a legal requirement, but it will protect your head if you fall.

In general it is a good idea to wear bright clothing so that you can be easily seen by motorists, and this is particularly important when it is overcast or getting dark. If you might be out in the dark or twilight fit your bicycle with lights — by law your bicycle must have a reflector. You can also buy reflective bands for your ankles, or to wear over your shoulder and back, and these help motorists to see you.

You may be surprised how quickly you use up energy when cycling, and it is important to eat a carbohydrate meal before you set out. When planning a long ride, eat well the night before. You should eat small amounts of food regularly while you are cycling, or you may find that your energy suddenly disappears, particularly if there are hills or if the weather is cold. It is important to always carry something to eat with you — chocolate, bananas, biscuits — so that if you do start fading away you can restore yourself quickly. In warm weather you will sweat and use up fluid, and you always need to carry something to drink — water will do! Many bicycles have a fitment in which to put a water bottle, and if you don't have one a cycle shop should be able to fit one.

It is also a good idea to carry a small first aid kit. This should include elastoplasts or bandages, sunburn cream, and an anti-histamine in case you are stung by a passing insect.

It is a good idea to have a pannier to carry all these items. Some fit on the handlebars, some to the back of the seat and some onto a back rack. For a day's ride you probably won't need a lot of carrying capacity, but it is better to carry items in a pannier rather than in a rucksack on your back. Pack items that you are carrying carefully — loose items can be dangerous.

Getting to the start of the ride

If you are lucky you will be able to cycle to the start of the ride, but often transport is necessary. If you travel there by train, some sprinter services carry two bicycles without prior booking. Other services carry bicycles free in off-peak periods, but check the details with your local station. Alternatively, you could use your car — it may be possible to get a bike in the back of a hatchback if you take out the front wheel. There are inexpensive, easily fitted car racks which carry bicycles safely. Your local cycle store will be able to supply one to suit you.

Cycling on-road

Cycling on back roads is a delight with quiet lanes, interesting villages, good views and smooth easy surface to coast along on. The cycle rides in this book are mainly on quiet roads but you sometimes cross busy roads or have stretches on B roads, and whatever sort of road you are on it is essential to ride safely. Always be aware of the possibility or existence of other traffic. Glance behind regularly, signal before you turn or change lane, and keep to the left. If there are motorists around, make sure that they have seen you before you cross their path. Cycling can be dangerous if you are competing for space with motor vehicles, many of which seem to have difficulty in seeing cyclists. When drivers are coming out of side

Crummock Water

oads, catch their eye before you ride in front of hem.

You will find that many roads have potholes and uneven edges. They are much more difficult to spot when you are in a group because of the restricted view ahead, and therefore warnings need to be given. It is a good idea to cycle about a metre out into the road, conditions permitting, so that you avoid the worst of the uneven surfaces and to give you room to move in to the left if you are closely overtaken by a motor vehicle.

Other things to be careful of are slippery roads, particularly where there is mud or fallen leaves. Sudden rain after a period of dry weather often makes the roads extremely slippery. Dogs, too, are a hazard because they often move unpredictably, and sometimes like to chase cyclists. If you are not happy, stop or go slowly until the problem has passed.

Pedalling

Many modern bikes have 18 or 21 gears with three rings at the front and six or seven on the back wheel, and for much of the time you will find that the middle gear at the front with the range of gears at the back will be fine. Use your gears to find one that is easy to pedal along in so that your feet move round easily and you do not put too much pressure on your knees. If you are new to the bike and the gears it is a good idea to practise changing the gears on a stretch of flat, quiet road so that when you need to change gears quickly you will be ready to do so.

Cycling in a group

When cycling in a group it is essential to do so in a disciplined manner for your own, and others', safety. Do not ride too close to the bicycle in front of you – keep about a bicycle's length between you so that you will have space to brake or stop. Always keep both hands on the handlebars, except when signalling, etc. It is alright to cycle two abreast on quiet roads, but if it is necessary to change from cycling two abreast to single file this is usually done by the outside rider falling in behind the nearside rider; always cycle in single file where there are double white lines, on busy roads, or on narrow and winding roads where you have a restricted view of the road ahead. Overtake on the right (outside) only; do not overtake on the inside.

It is important to pass information to other members of the group, for example:

car up – a vehicle is coming up behind the group and will be overtaking;

car down – a vehicle is coming towards the group;

single up – get into single file;

stopping – stopping, or

slowing/easy – slowing due to junction, etc., ahead;

on the left – there is an obstacle on the left, e.g. pedestrian, parked car;

pothole – pothole (and point towards it).

Accidents

In case of an accident, stay calm and, if needed, ring the emergency services on 999. It is a good idea to carry a basic first aid kit and perhaps also one of the commercial foil wraps to put around anyone who has an accident to keep them warm. If someone comes off their bicycle move them and the bike off the road if it is safe to do so. Get someone in the party to warn approaching traffic to slow down, and if necessary ring for an ambulance.

Cycling off-road

All the routes in this book take you along legal rights of way – bridleways, byways open to all traffic and roads used as public paths – it is illegal to cycle along footpaths. Generally the off-road sections of the routes will be easy if the weather and ground are dry. If the weather has been wet and the ground is muddy, it is not a good idea to cycle along bridleways unless you do not mind getting dirty and unless you have a mountain bike which will not get blocked up with mud. In dry weather any bicycle will be able to cover the bridleway sections, but you may need to dismount if the path is very uneven.

Off-road cycling is different to cycling on the road. The average speed is lower, you will use more energy, your riding style will be different and there is a different set of rules to obey – the off-road code:

1 Give way to horse riders and pedestrians and use a bell or call out to warn someone of your presence.

2 Take your rubbish with you.

3 Do not light fires.

4 Close gates behind you.

5 Do not interfere with wildlife, plants or trees.

6 Use only tracks where you have a right of way, or where the landowner has given you permission to ride.

7 Avoid back wheel skids, which can start erosion gulleys and ruin the bridleway.

Some of the off-road rides take you some miles from shelter and civilisation – take waterproofs, plenty of food and drink and basic tools especially spare inner tubes and tyre repair equipment. Tell someone where you are going and approximately when you are due back. You are more likely to tumble off your bike riding off road, so you should consider wearing a helmet and mittens with padded palms.

Local Tourist Information Centres

Ambleside
The Old Courthouse, Church Street, Ambleside
Telephone (015394) 32582

Appleby
Moot Hall, Boroughgate, Appleby
Telephone (017683) 51177

Broughton-in-Furness
Old Town Hall, The Square, Broughton-in-Furness
Telephone (01229) 716115

Carlisle
Old Town Hall, Greenmarket, Carlisle
Telephone (01228) 512444

Cockermouth
Town Hall, Market Street, Cockermouth
Telephone (01900) 822634

Coniston
Ruskin Avenue, Coniston
Telephone (015394) 41533

Egremont
Lowes Court Gallery, Main Street, Egremont
Telephone (01946) 820693

Grange-over-Sands
Victoria Hall, Main Street, Grange-over-Sands
Telephone (015395) 34026

Grasmere
Red Bank Road, Grasmere
Telephone (015394) 35245

Hawkshead
Main Car Park, Hawkshead
Telephone (015394) 36525

Kendal
Town Hall, Highgate, Kendal
Telephone (01539) 725758

Keswick
Moot Hall, Market Square, Keswick
Telephone (017687) 72645

Kirkby Lonsdale
24 Main Street, Kirkby Lonsdale
Telephone (015242) 71437

Kirkby Stephen
Market Street, Kirkby Stephen
Telephone (017683) 71199

Maryport
Maritime Museum, Senhouse Street, Maryport
Telephone (01900) 813738

Penrith
Middlegate, Penrith
Telephone (01768) 867466

Sedbergh
72 Main Street, Sedbergh
Telephone (015396) 20125

Ulverston
Coronation Hall, County Square, Ulverston
Telephone (01229) 587120

Windermere
Victoria Street, Windermere
Telephone (015394) 46499

Local cycle hire

Eden Bikes
The Sands, Appleby
Telephone (017683) 53533

Keswick Motor Company
Lake Road, Keswick
Telephone (017687) 72064

Keswick Mountain Bike Centre
Dalston Court, Southey Hill Trading Estate, Keswick
Telephone (017687) 75202

Mortlake Mountain Bikes
32/34 Market Street, Kirkby Stephen
Telephone (017683) 71666

North Lakes Bike Hire
Lakeshore, Derwentwater Marina
Telephone (016973) 71871

Robinsons
2 Market Street, Kirkby Stephen
Telephone (017683) 71519

The Stores and Post Office, Orton
Telephone (015396) 24225

Summitreks
14 Yewdale Road, Coniston
Telephone (015394) 41212

Mark Taylor Cycles
5-6 New Street, Whitehaven
Telephone (01946) 692252

Local cycle shops

Eden Bikes, Keswick Mountain Bike Centre, Robinsons and
Mark Taylor Cycles.

Derwent Cycles
4 Market Place, Cockermouth
Telephone (01900) 822113

Eric Hindmoor
18 Wood Street, Maryport
Telephone (01900) 812231

The New Bike Shop
18-20 Market Place, Workington
Telephone (01900) 603337

KESWICK AND CASTLERIGG STONE CIRCLE

Route information

Distance 11km (7 miles)

Grade Moderate

Terrain Short, steep section after Keswick. Otherwise well-surfaced track. Suitable for all types of bicycle.

Time to allow 1–3 hours.

Getting there by car Keswick is on the A66, Penrith to Workington road. Drive to the town centre and park in the signed long stay car park on Otley Road.

Getting there by train There is no practical railway access to this ride.

From Keswick eastwards on a short stretch of busy road. The route quickly turns onto a quiet lane with a sharp climb to Castlerigg Stone Circle. The return route descends to the bed of an old railway track, for a level well-surfaced return to Keswick.

Places of interest along the route

Ⓐ Cars of the Stars Motor Museum, Keswick

Situated in the town centre, Cars of the Stars features TV and film vehicles. See Chitty Chitty Bang Bang, FAB1, the Thunderbirds Rolls Royce, the Batmobile and many other famous cars and motorbikes. Also film set displays and vehicles. Open Easter to November, New Year and February school half term, daily 1000–1700; also December, weekends only 1000–1700. Charge. Telephone (017687) 73757.

Ⓑ Castlerigg Stone Circle

There are around 40 stone circles still in existence in Cumbria – Castlerigg is the best preserved. Thirty-eight stones (33 still standing) make up the circle and a further ten stones stand in a rectangle. Castlerigg is thought to have been constructed around 3000 BC. The views of the fells, especially towards Blencathra, are spectacular and the site makes a good picnic spot. National Trust property. Open at all reasonable times. Admission by donation. Telephone the National Trust on (015394) 35599 for further information.

Ⓒ Cockermouth, Keswick and Penrith Railway

Construction started on 21 May 1862 and the railway was opened in November 1864. The track was 49.5km (31 miles) long and had 135 bridges. It was built to carry coal and steel, but this declined as tourism increased – in 1913 the railway carried 482,000 people. Due to falling demand, the railway was finally closed in 1972. Part of the old track bed has been opened as a footpath/cycleway. There are numerous gates but this has had the advantage of discouraging cycling clubs, leaving the route for slower recreational cyclists. The bridges and adjacent River Greta add to the charm.

Keswick Museum and Art Gallery, Fitz Park

Passed on your return into Keswick, this is the Lake District's only purpose built Victorian Museum and Art Gallery. Displays include material on the Lakeland poets, musical stones and a 500-year-old cat. Changing exhibitions by local artists. Open Easter to October, daily 1000–1600. Charge. Telephone (017687) 73263.

Castlerigg Stone Circle

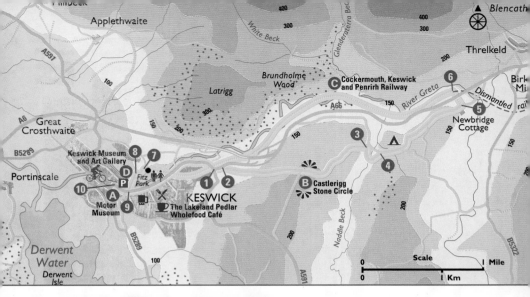

Route description

Leave Otley Road car park and TL into Otley Road. TL into Victoria Street (opposite the short stay car park). Pass the motor museum on the right, continue through the traffic lights, SP Windermere, and along the road with Fitz Park on the left.

1 TL, SP Castlerigg stone circle.

2 TR onto Eleven Trees Road, SP Castlerigg Stone Circle. Quite a steep climb brings you to the entrance of the stone circle on the right. Carefully descend to the TJ.

3 TR at TJ, SP Grasmere.

4 TR at TJ, SP Grasmere. Pass Burns campsite on the left. Take care now, as the descent is steep and narrow.

5 TL, SP Railway Footpath. This turn is easily missed – at the bottom of the hill opposite Newbridge cottage (white house) is the gate leading to the railway path. Ride along the narrow track to another gate.

5.5km (3.5 miles)

6 TL at TJ, no SP (right is over a bridge). The route now follows the old railway track, alongside the River Greta. Look out for the various

interpretive signs about the valley as you cross bridges and pass through gates. Construction of the A66 destroyed one of the tunnels and you have to climb up over a bank and descend under a flyover to rejoin the track on the other side. Shortly after this point great care should be taken as the path drops steeply and unexpectedly for 30m, before continuing to the old Keswick station.

7 TL at the far end of the platform, keeping the row of eight metal bollards to your right. Follow this path which turns right to the front entrance of the leisure pool.

8 Descend to the road and TR. Then SO at TJ 10m further on, into Station road. To the left is a bowling green, to the right Keswick Museum and Art Gallery **10.5km (6.5 miles)**

9 TR at XR, SP Town Centre.

10 Rejoining outward route, TR into Otley Road and return to the car park and the end of the route. **11km (7 miles)**

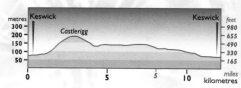

ARNSIDE AND MILNTHORPE – THE KENT ESTUARY

Route information

Distance 17km (10.5 miles)

Grade Moderate

Terrain Undulating lanes and some waymarked off-road riding. The return to Arnside is via the relatively flat coastal road. Bikes with low gears advisable for the climb up to Arnside Knott and for the off-road section of the route.

Time to allow 2–3 hours.

Getting there by car Arnside is on the B5282, 6.5km (4 miles) west of Milnthorpe, which is on the A6 north of Carnforth (junction 35, M6).

Getting there by train Arnside has a railway station, on the Barrow Line. Telephone (0345) 484950 for information.

This ride provides an opportunity to explore the National Trust's woodland on Arnside Knott, with splendid views to the south towards Silverdale, the Kent estuary and Morecambe; and to the northwest the Keer estuary and across Morecambe Bay to Grange-over-Sands and the fells of the southern Lake District. It also provides gently rolling limestone scenery, which remains relatively unspoiled and has an abundance of wildlife.

Places of interest along the route

Ⓐ Arnside Knott, near Arnside

Arnside Knott is a limestone headland of old woodland and wild flowers. It is owned by the National Trust and is part of the Arnside and Silverdale Area of Outstanding Natural Beauty. The headland rises 1709m (521 feet) above sea level. Good views of the Lakeland Fells, the Pennines and the coast. Accessible at all reasonable times.

Ⓑ Milnthorpe

The town's origin and development owe much to the presence of the River Bela and the nearby Kent Estuary, as they provided both transport and power. The mills had their heyday between 1740 and 1840, when raw materials were brought directly by boat. The market square (where there has been a market since 1334) is a conservation area. **Dallam Park**, with sheep, deer and a large number of water birds, was the 18th-century landscaped deer park of Dallam Tower, a Queen Anne style house. A network of paths run through the wooded countryside. Access at all reasonable times.

Ⓒ Kent Railway Viaduct

This landmark crosses the sands between Arnside and Grange-over-Sands, over the Kent Estuary.

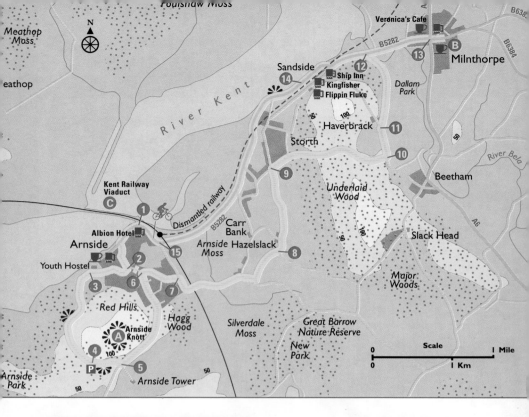

Route description

From Arnside Pier/Post Office, ride to the southern end of the seafront.

1 TL at Albion Hotel into Silverdale Road, SP Arnside Knott, and climb the hill.

2 TR into Redhills Road and follow signs to Arnside Knott, passing Arnside Youth Hostel.

3 Continue up steep gradient, SP Arnside Knott. After a cattle grid, the road becomes a rough track from which there are splendid views over the estuary to Grange.

4 At car park, take waymarked bridleway (exit to left of car park). Follow bridleway and exit wood after approximately 1.5km (1 mile). (Waymarking, on all gates, is by a green National Trust sign with a cyclist superimposed on the arrow.)

To avoid the off-road section, retrace the route from Arnside Knott car park to direction 2 where, at foot of hill, TR past the youth hostel. Continue to end of Redhills Road and TR at TJ then take first left, rejoining the main route in Briery Bank, SP Yealand and Carnforth (direction 6).

5 TL towards Arnside at minor road (Silverdale to Arnside), opposite track leading to Arnside Tower. Ignore right turns until Briery Bank. **4km (2.5 miles)**

6 TR into Briery Bank, SP Yealand and Carnforth. Descend hill with care.

7 TR at TJ, SP Silverdale and Carnforth. Cross railway.

8 TL, SP Storth, and continue to Storth XR.

9 TR at XR, SP Beetham. Follow Cockshut Lane through woods to TJ.

10 TL at TJ, towards Haverbrack (no SP).

11 TR by trees at gated road (lodge to left of gates), no SP, into Dallam Park (10.5km/6.5 miles). Continue to TJ with B5282, Arnside/Milnthorpe road.

12 TR at TJ, into Milnthorpe. The market square is just beyond the traffic lights, to the right.

13 Exit Milnthorpe on the B5282, retracing route. At direction 12 continue towards Arnside.

14 Continue through Sandside and towards Arnside.

15 TR at TJ, continue past the railway station and onto the seafront and the end of the route. *17km (10.5 miles)*

Food and drink

Arnside has a number of pubs and cafés on the seafront. En route, there are several pubs and cafés in Milnthorpe, centred on the town square to the east of the A6 traffic lights. Also pubs serving food in Sandside.

Veronica's Café, Milnthorpe
Teas, coffees and snacks, en route. Also local tourist information point.

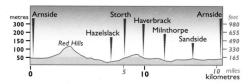

Arnside Knott

WORDSWORTH COUNTRY – GRASMERE, ELTERWATER, RYDAL

Route information

Distance 17.5km (11 miles)

Grade Moderate

Terrain One steep tarmacked climb and two beautiful off-road sections that are rocky in places. Suitable for mountain bikes.

Time to allow 2–4 hours.

Getting there by car Grasmere is off the A591, Keswick to Windermere road. Park in the Stock Lane car park, on the B5287.

Getting there by train There is no practical railway access to this ride.

The initial steep climb out of Grasmere and up Red Bank provides wonderful views south before the route descends into Elterwater via Chapel Stile. The route continues past Loughrigg Tarn and onto a moderate section of wide off-road cycling below Loughrigg Fell. Then onto Rydal, with a chance to visit Wordsworth's house at Rydal Mount, before following the coffin route along a mostly well-graded track to Dove Cottage in Grasmere. There are several good picnic stops along this route (all indicated on the map): just past High Close Youth Hostel, 500m along old coffin road; between directions 12 and 13, beside stepping stones over the River Rothay.

Route description

Leaving Stock Lane car park, TR towards the centre of Grasmere. Opposite the church TL, SP Tourist Information. Pass Red Bank Road car park and the Tourist Information Centre on the left and continue along a narrow lane, past the boating station on the left. Steep climb ahead, up Red Bank.

1 TR, SP Youth hostel. Continue uphill from the junction to pass High Close Youth Hostel on the left. Descent into Chapel Stile, with beautiful views of Elterwater and the fells.

2 TL opposite the church entrance and continue down the hill. ***5km (3 miles)***

3 Arrive at TJ on the B5343, TL no SP. On the left is Langdale village store. Cycle on passing Wainwrights Inn.

4 TR, SP Elterwater.

5 Arrive Elterwater. TL at TJ opposite the bowling club, SP Ambleside.

6 TR at TJ with B5343, no SP. Take care on this fast road.

7 TL, no SP. Pass a width restriction sign.

8 TR at TJ, SP Ambleside. Downhill, at an apparent junction, bear left keeping to the road.

9 TL almost immediately, opposite a post box in the wall, and head up along tarmac towards farm buildings.

10 The first section of off-road starts here. After 50 m (just before entering the yard) TR, SP Footpath to Tarn. SO at the footpath XR, 100m later. Follow the blue arrow on yellow sign. ***9km (5.5 miles)***

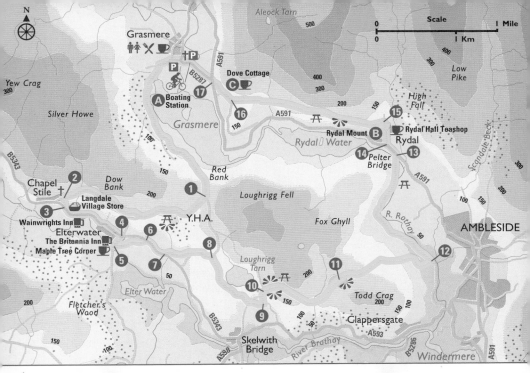

11 A steep stony climb leads to a wooden gate which you pass through, SP Ambleside. Bear right when the track splits, following the wall on the right. Cross a stream, through a gate and descend, through High Barn onto tarmac and a steep descent with Ambleside ahead.

12 TL at TJ just over a cattle grid, no SP. Continue along the valley, following the River Rothay.

13 Cross Pelter Bridge to TJ with the A591, where TL. Take care, this is a fast road – there is a good pavement, so it may be better to walk.

14 TR, SP Rydal Mount. Continue uphill, passing the entrance to Rydal Hall Teashop on the right and Rydal Mount on the left. Continue upwards on the steep concrete road (a curved tarmac section goes to the right, avoiding this extreme gradient).

15 TL, SP Public Bridleway Grasmere. Go through a gate and along a generally well-surfaced track (midway, there is one rocky, steep section). This was originally a coffin route, used to carry coffins from Rydal to Grasmere. There are great views over the lakes to the left. Pass Brockstone cottage and shortly tarmac begins.

14.5km (9 miles)

16 TR at TJ, no SP (opposite a barn). Pass Dove Cottage on the right.

17 TR at staggered XR, then TL, SP Grasmere village and return to the car park.

17.5km (11 miles)

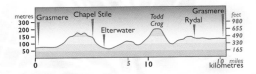

Places of interest along the route

Ⓐ Boating Station, Grasmere Lake
Rowing boats for hire. Also ice creams, sweets and teas. For information, telephone Grasmere Tourist Information Centre on (015394) 35245.

Ⓑ Rydal Mount, Ambleside
Rydal Mount was the home of William Wordsworth between 1813 and 1850 and is today owned by his descendants. The house contains portraits, personal possessions and first editions of Wordsworth's work, and visitors can see rooms that have changed little since Wordsworth's day. Garden. Open March to October, daily 0930–1700; November to February, Wednesday–Monday 1000–1600. Charge. Telephone (015394) 33002.

Ⓒ Dove Cottage
Dove Cottage was William Wordsworth's home between 1799 and 1808. Guided tours available of the house and (weather permitting) the garden. Also the award-winning Wordsworth Museum displaying a unique collection of manuscripts, books and paintings interpreting the

Food and drink

There are numerous eateries in Grasmere, and village shops in Chapel Stile and Elterwater.

Wainwrights Inn, Great Langdale
A traditional Cumbrian pub serving bar meals.

The Britannia Inn, Elterwater
Hotel and pub. Real ales, lunches, afternoon teas and evening meals.

Rydal Hall Teashop, Rydal
Reached along a short track, a basic tearoom with the added attraction of a nearby waterfall.

life and work of Wordsworth. Changing exhibitions. Gift shop and tearoom (serving evening meals July and August). Open all year, daily 0930–1730. Charge (discount ticket with Rydal Mount and Wordsworth House, Cockermouth – see Route 4). Telephone (015394) 35544.

Grasmere

COCKERMOUTH AND THE NORTHERN FELLS

Route information

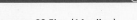

Distance 22.5km (14 miles)

Grade Moderate

Terrain A converted railway track, flat roads and one steep climb, all of which are suitable for most bikes.

Time to allow 2–3 hours, although you could take a whole day.

Getting there by car Cockermouth is along the A595, off the A66 Penrith to Workington road. There are two main car parks in town – this ride starts from the car park next to the Tourist Information Centre.

Getting there by train There is no practical railway access to this ride.

Out of Cockermouth on the Greenway, a well-surfaced reclaimed railway line. Then onto a quiet, undulating road through Wythop and to the edge of Bassenthwaite Lake, where you can picnic by the shore. There is an optional visit to an animal park, before returning to Cockermouth via the only longish hill of the day. However, the views of the northern fells and the descent to Cockermouth make it worthwhile.

Places of interest along the route

Ⓐ Cockermouth

The historic town of Cockermouth sits at the point where the River Cocker joins the River Derwent. The **Cumberland Toy and Model Museum**, Banks Court, Market Place, exhibits mainly British toys of the 20th century. There are visitor-operated displays including vintage trains, Scalextric cars and Lego models. Open February to November, daily 1000–1700. Charge. Telephone (01900) 827606. **Aspects of Motoring** is housed within Jennings Brewery and contains vintage and veteran cars, motorcycles and displays on motorsport. Coffee shop. Open March to October, daily 1000–1600; November, December and February, weekends and school half term 1000–1600. Charge. Telephone (01900) 824448. **Jennings Brewery** has been producing traditional beers for over 160 years. Brewery tours March to October, weekdays; April to September, also Saturdays. Charge. Telephone to confirm times on (01900) 821011. **Wordsworth House**, Main Street, is the birthplace of William Wordsworth. Seven rooms are furnished in 18th-century style and there are a number of Wordsworth's personal effects. Gift shop and restaurant. National Trust property. Open March to October, Monday– Friday 1100–1700; June to September also Saturdays. Charge (discount ticket available in conjunction with Dove Cottage and Rydal Mount – see Route 3). Telephone (01900) 824805. The **Museum of Printing** is open all year, Monday–Saturday 1000–1600. Charge. Telephone (01900) 824984. The **Mining Museum** is open April to December, Monday–Saturday 1000–1700. Nominal charge. Telephone (01900) 828301.

Ⓑ Trotters and Friends Animal Farm, Coalbeck Farm, Bassenthwaite

Rare breeds, traditional farm animals, endangered species, birds of prey and reptiles can all be seen. Hands-on activities such as milking a cow and exercising the animals. Children's play areas. Gift shop and tearoom. Open March to October, daily 1000–1730; November to February, 1000–1630. Charge. Telephone (017687) 76239.

ⓒ Ouse Bridge Nature Reserve

Stone steps lead down to a stony beach, providing the best example of rock shoreline vegetation in the national park. An excellent place for a picnic.

Bassenthwaite Lake

Food and drink

There are several pubs and teashops in Cockermouth.

🛏 The Pheasant, Bassenthwaite Lake
Hotel and bar in old coaching inn. Morning coffee, lunches and afternoon teas.

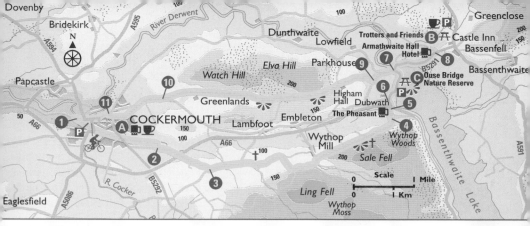

Route description

From the car park by the Tourist Information Centre, exit and TL into market place, 10m later TL at the TJ, SP Wordsworth House. Directly in front is an alleyway leading to Banks Court, which contains the Cumberland Toy and Model Museum, Aspects of Motoring and Jennings Brewery. Continue along main street, passing the shops on both sides. SO at mini roundabout (on the right Wordsworth's House). Cycle along Crown Street to the next mini roundabout where SO.

1 TL into Horseman Street. Cycle to the end of the street and up the tarmac zig zag onto the Greenway cyclepath. (The cyclepath meets a carpark below a school – cycle across the car park with the school on your right, cross the road and follow the narrow cyclepath to the war memorial on your left. The cycleway continues by the wall on the other side of the road, SP No Motorcycles.) The cyclepath is now easy to follow as you take the signs for Strawberry How.

2 TL at TJ at the end of the cyclepath, opposite Strawberry How Business Centre. Cross the A66.

3 TL at TJ, SP Embleton. Pass St Cuthbert's church on the left and cycle into Wythop Mill. Take care – steep downhill gradient. Continue along undulating road to reach the high point (with Wythop church on the right). Care on the rapid descent. **4.5km (3 miles)**

4 TL at TJ, SP Embleton. TL at TJ 100m further on, SP Castle Inn. **10.5km (6.5 miles)**

5 Take care as you arrive at the A66. SO (staggered XR), SP Castle Inn.

6 TR, SP Castle Inn. (The brown sheep sign is for Trotters and Friends.) Pass the car park for Ouse Bridge Nature Reserve on the right.

7 TL at TJ and continue to direction 9. To visit Trotters and Friends, TR at this junction over the bridge, SP Castle Inn. Carry on for 1km (0.6 mile) to TL by the Armathwaite Hall Hotel.

8 It is 0.5km (0.3 miles) to Trotters and Friends from here – follow the sheep signs. Retrace your route to direction 7 and continue on to direction 9.

9 TR by the triangle of grass, SP Higham Hall. Climb the only severe hill of the ride – great views of the northern fells

10 Arrive at the TJ and TR, no SP. **19km (12 miles)**

11 Pass the Cockermouth sign. TL, no SP. Descend into town (car park and Tourist Information Centre on left) to the end of the route. **22.5km (14 miles)**

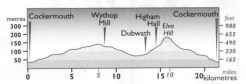

CARLISLE AND ROCKCLIFFE LOOP

Route information

Distance 22.5km (14 miles)

Grade Easy

Terrain Mostly flat, initially on a cyclepath out of Carlisle, after which quiet country lanes.

Time to allow 2–3 hours.

Getting there by car Carlisle is reached from the M6. There is ample parking in the centre with the two car parks on either side of the castle particularly convenient.

Getting there by train Carlisle is served by regular services from all over the country. Telephone (0345) 484950.

Leaving Carlisle over the Eden Bridge, the route follows a series of quiet lanes to the pretty village of Rockcliffe, where there is an excellent picnic spot, and then returns to Carlisle via a nature reserve.

Places of interest along the route

A Carlisle

Carlisle, in the borderland between England and Scotland, has witnessed hundreds of years of history. **Carlisle Castle**, a medieval fortress, has ancient chambers, stairways and dungeons to explore. Exhibition offers an insight to William Rufus, Mary Queen of Scots and Bonnie Prince Charlie. Panoramic views of the city itself and the hills of the Lake District and southern Scotland. Guided tours. Gift shop. English Heritage property. Open April to September, daily 0930–1800; October to March, daily 1000–1600. Charge (included in the admission price is entrance to the King's Own Royal Border Regiment Museum). Telephone (01228) 591922. **Tullie House**, an award-winning museum and art gallery, describes the history of Carlisle and the Borders. Journey through time, from the Roman occupation, to the Middle Ages and on to the Edwardian era. Interactive exhibitions and craft workshops. Gift shop and restaurant. Open all year, Monday–Saturday 1000–1700; Sunday 1200–1700. Charge. Telephone (01228) 34781. **Carlisle Cathedral** was founded in 1122 – despite the border warfare, services have been said in it daily for nearly 900 years. Many items of interest, including stained glass from the 14th through to the 20th century. Gift shop and restaurant. Open all year, daily 0730–1830. Admission by donation. Telephone (01228) 48151.

B Kingmoor Nature Trail

Northwest of Carlisle, this was the Kings Moor, granted to the people of Carlisle by Edward III in 1352. The nature trail largely follows the line of a race course, used for centuries until around 1850. Woodland, clearings, wild flowers and birds. Access at all reasonable times. Admission free. Telephone (01228) 23411 for further information.

Route description

Start from Castleway, on the cyclepath on the castle-side of the road (Tullie House opposite). Cycle down the path with the castle on the left, cross the road leading to car park and continue round left and over Eden bridge.

1 TL into Cavendish Terrace. Cycle the tree-lined road and pass through the small path at the end.

2 TL at TJ, SP Kingstown (cycle sign).

3 TL into Etterby Road (by phone box). Cycle through residential area and round a sharp right bend.

4 TR by Stainton sign. Cycle up hill.

5 TL at TJ, no SP. Pass the hangers of Cargo Village. *4.5km (3 miles)*

6 TL at TJ, SP Rockcliffe.

7 Enter Rockcliffe and TL as the road bends to the right (opposite the church). Take care as the road drops down over a bridge. Pass a great picnic area on the left, then climb a short hill.

8 TL at TJ, no SP. *9.5km (6 miles)*

9 TL, SP Rockcliffe Cross. Cycle through pleasant farming country, past a telephone box and post box.

10 TR, no SP.

11 TR at TJ, SP Rockcliffe, and cycle back through Rockcliffe.

12 TR at end of village, SP Cargo. Retrace your route back past Cargo. On the edge of Carlisle, TL (by the 30 mph speed sign) to Kingmoor Nature Trail.

13 TR, SP City centre (blue cycle sign).

14 Retrace your route along Cavendish terrace and then to the castle.

22.5km (14 miles)

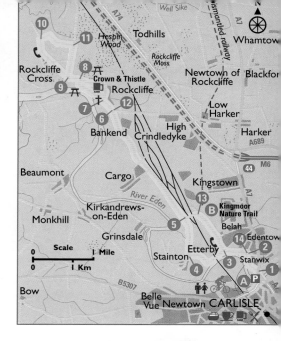

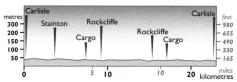

Food and drink

There are plenty of places to eat and drink in Carlisle.

Crown and Thistle, Rockcliffe
Open at lunchtime and in the evening. Outdoor seating.

HISTORIC PENRITH, LOWTHER AND BROUGHAM

Route information

Distance 26.5km (16.5 miles)

Grade Easy

Terrain Flat, except for a steep section of 2.5km (1.5 miles) through Lowther Park.

Time to allow 2 hours – all day.

Getting there by car For Penrith leave the M6 at Junction 40. This route starts by the Tourist Information Centre.

Getting there by train Penrith is on the London–Glasgow Intercity line. Telephone (0345) 484950 for information.

A quiet route is taken out of Penrith. Over the next 24km (15 miles), you will pass eight interesting attractions, for the most part on quiet flat roads. You may wish to stop at none, or make a day of it and visit most of them. Penrith Castle is open late so can be left until last. The only hard piece of cycling is through Lowther Park, but the views here make this seem insignificant.

Places of interest along the route

A Penrith

Penrith was the capital of Cumbria in the 9th and 10th centuries and, until 1070 AD was part of the Kingdom of Scotland and Strathclyde.

There is a wealth of historic building around the town. **St Andrew's Church** was established in 1133 and the tower is all that remains of the medieval building. The church nave was rebuilt between 1719 and 1722 after the earlier building had been damaged by fire. In the churchyard is the Giant's Grave (two 11th-century crosses and four hogback gravestones) and the Giant's Thumb (another pre-Norman cross). Construction on **Penrith Castle** was begun in 1399 and it was improved and added to over the 70 years, until it became a royal fortress for Richard, Duke of Gloucester, in his role as the 'Guardian of the west march towards Scotland'. The castle is now an empty but impressive shell, much of the original stone having been used as building material elsewhere in the town. Access at all reasonable times. The **Clock Tower**, in Market Square in the centre of town, was built in 1816 to commemorate the death of Philip Musgrave of Eden Hall. The tower stands on the site of the old Market Cross. **Penrith Museum**, situated next to the Tourist Information Centre in a 300-year-old school building, describes the area's fascinating past with exhibits and artefacts. Open June to September, Monday–Saturday 0930–1800, Sunday 1300–1800; October to May, Monday–Saturday 1000–1700. Telephone (01768) 212228.

B Brougham Castle

Brougham Castle, now operated by English Heritage, was a prized possession of Lady Anne Clifford. The castle dates from the 14th century and in 1653 Lady Anne began restoration of the building. She died here in 1676. The castle was built on the site of a Roman fort, *Brocavum*, and there are a number of Roman tombstones to be seen. Picnic in the grounds. Open April to October, daily 1000–1800 (or dusk if earlier); during October closed daily 1300–1400. Charge. Telephone (01768) 62488.

ⓒ Brougham Hall

There has been a fortified building on this site since circa 1480. During the 19th century, the Hall was known as the Windsor of the North and was the home of the Lord Chancellor of England. King Edward VII and the future King George V used Brougham Hall as a half-way house between Windsor and Balmoral. The hall gradually fell into dereliction until 1985, when restoration was started. Museum with exhibits on the history of Brougham and the surrounding area. Visitors can see the Cromwellian Chapel and the Main Hall. The site is now home to a variety of craft workshops, including wood-turners, chocolate makers and jewellers. Tearoom. The site is open all year round, daily, but the opening times of the individual workshops vary. Admission to workshops free; admission to Chapel and main hall by donation. Telephone Brougham Hall Charitable Trust on (01768) 868184 for further information.

ⓓ King Arthur's Round Table

A prehistoric meeting place dating from circa 2000–1000 BC. There was a burial mound at the centre of the site. Access at all reasonable times.

ⓔ Mayburgh Henge

With a diameter of 120m (394 feet), there is a single standing stone in the centre of this henge. Access at all reasonable times.

ⓕ Lowther Castle and Lakeland Bird of Prey Centre

Built between 1806 and 1811, only the façade of Lowther Castle remains. The Lakeland Bird of Prey Centre is situated in the walled garden of the castle, surrounded by unspoilt parkland. Visitors can see many species of birds at close quarters. Tearoom and garden. Open March to October, daily 1030–dusk. Flying demonstrations

Brougham Castle

daily at 1200, 1400 and 1600. Charge. Telephone (01931) 712746.

G Lowther Park

This leisure and wildlife park is set in 61ha (150 acres) of parkland. The theme park has family rides, adventure play areas, a miniature railway and a boating lake. There is regular live entertainment with an international circus show and puppet theatre. The wildlife area is home to familiar and exotic animals and birds. Restaurant. Open all year, daily 1000–1700 (dusk if earlier). Charge. Telephone (01931) 712523.

H Wetheriggs Pottery

Wetheriggs is the UK's only steam-powered pottery. Watch craftsmen at work or have a go a throwing a pot yourself. Also museum, pottery and craft shop, rare breeds of pig and nature area. Children's play area and tearoom. Open all year, daily 1000–1700. Charge. Telephone (01768) 892733.

Food and drink

There are numerous places for refreshment in Penrith.

Queens Parlour Tearoom and Queens Head Inn, Askham
Pub, hotel and tearooms. Meals served all day. Outdoor seating.

Punchbowl Inn, Askham
Restaurant meals.

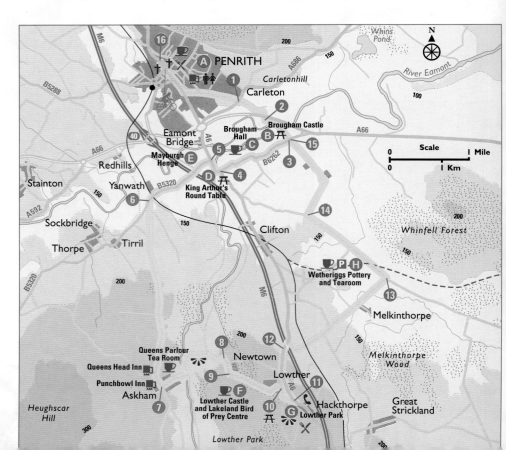

Route description

Start on Middlegate, by the Tourist Information Centre and cycle to the clock tower, via the one way system. (TL here to visit St Andrews Church or TR into Cornmarket and cycle up the hill to visit the castle.) Otherwise, continue past the clock tower and TL into Roper Street (after Old London Road, which is signed). Follow Roper Street as it turns into Carleton road. Continue to staggered XR (opposite the Cross Keys pub).

1 SO at XR, SP Cross Keys. Cycle down the dead end road, through the gate and walk along the wide public footpath, under the A66 to the TJ where TL, no SP.

2 TR at TJ. Note – a mistake here would take you onto the A66. Pass the entrance to Brougham Castle on the right.

3 TR at XR, SP Brougham Hall. Pass Brougham Hall.

4 TR at TJ, SP Penrith. Take care on the A6 – you can walk along the pavement here if you feel the traffic is too busy.

5 TL, SP Tirril (5.5km/3.5 miles). Pass King Arthur's Round Table and continue past Yanwath.

6 TL, SP Askham.

7 Arrive at Askham and TL, SP Lowther. This is the prettiest part of the ride, but also the hardest. Care should be taken on the steep descent to a bridge leading into Lowther Park. Once over the bridge the road climbs quite steeply through the grounds, with Lowther Castle prominent on the right. **11km (7 miles)**

8 TR close to the top of the hill, SP Lowther.

9 TL at TJ, SP Lowther. Pass the houses of Newtown. On the right is the Lakeland Bird of Prey Centre.

10 Arrive at a TJ opposite Pennine Close where TR, no SP. Pass the entrance to Lowther Park on the right.

Askham

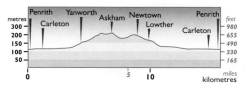

11 TL at TJ by a phone box, no SP, for a stretch of downhill along the A6.
15km (9.5 miles)

12 Cross the M6, immediately TR, SP Melkinthorpe.

13 TL at TJ, SP Penrith. Pass Wetheriggs Pottery on the left.

14 TR, SP Brougham. Continue past some farms. **21km (13 miles)**

15 SO at XR, SP Brougham Castle. You are now back on the same road used to exit Penrith. Retrace the route back to the town centre – TL, pass under the A66, walk the footpath, continue up the hill to the staggered XR, SO and TR at the end of Roper Street, SP Town Centre.

16 Continue to the Tourist Information Centre to complete the round trip.
26.5km (16.5 miles)

TROUTBECK AND TOWNEND, OFF-ROAD FROM AMBLESIDE

Route information

Distance 21.5km (13.5 miles)

Grade Moderate

Terrain Three sections of easy to moderate off-road riding, otherwise quiet lanes and a final section of reasonably busy A road (although the latter can be avoided by walking the pavement).

Time to allow 2–4 hours

Getting there by car Ambleside is on the north shore of Lake Windermere, on the A591 Windermere to Keswick road. Park in the Waterhead Car Park, from where the lake steamers leave. There is a Tourist Information Centre here.

Getting there by train The nearest railway station is Windermere, from where a bus service runs to Ambleside. Telephone (01946) 63222.

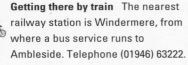

This route travels from Ambleside, over a section of off-road track (at times a rocky climb) to the wonderful views at Jenkin Crag. A reasonably flat traverse ensues before the descent into Troutbeck village. After a tour of the village, a second section of off-road (steep and rocky) takes you up to Dubbs Road. From here the route descends to Lake Windermere and the return to Ambleside.

Places of interest along the route

Ⓐ Stagshaw Garden, near Ambleside
Woodland garden with collections of azaleas and rhododendrons. Many trees and shrubs including magnolias, camellias and embothriums. National Trust property. Open April to June, daily 1000–1830. Charge. Telephone (015394) 35599.

Ⓑ Townend, near Ambleside
Townend is a preserved statesman farmer's (a wealthy yeoman's) house. It was built circa 1626 and contains carved woodwork, books, papers, furniture and historical implements, all collected by generations of the Browne family, who lived in the house from its construction until 1943. National Trust property. Open April to November, Tuesday–Friday, Sunday and Bank Holidays 1300–1700 (or dusk if earlier). Charge. Telephone (015394) 32628.

Ⓒ Brockhole Visitor Centre, Lake Windermere
The Lake District National Park was created in 1951 and covers 2292 square km (885 square miles). Brockhole Visitor Centre opened in 1969 and is set in 12ha (30 acres) of terraced gardens and grounds reaching down to the shores of Lake Windermere. Exhibitions and displays on the Lake District, regular film and slide shows and events. Restaurant and tearooms, adventure playground and picnic area. Cruises on Lake Windermere. Open March to November, daily 1000–1700. Gardens and grounds open all year, daily 1000–1700. Lake cruises available (subject to weather conditions) Easter week and May to September, daily 1110–1710. Telephone (015394) 46601.

Aerial view of Troutbeck

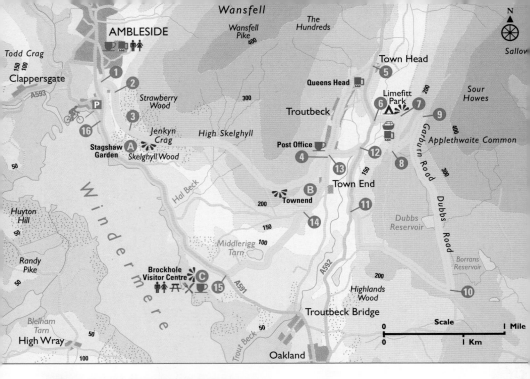

Route description

Leave the car park, from beside the Tourist Information Centre, and TL. TL at the traffic lights and then TL onto the A591. TR opposite the garden centre and up Old Lake Road.

1 TR, SP Jenkin Crag (the track is partly tarmacked).

2 TR, SP Jenkin Crag, onto the bridleway. The track degenerates to a rocky path after the last house. Pass the entrance to Skelghyll Wood on the right.

3 LHF, SP Jenkin Crag. This sign is for a footpath but it is a bridleway. Pass Stagshaw Garden on the right. The path is quite steep and rocky in places as you ascend to the entrance to Jenkin Crag on the right. Take time to look at the view over Windermere. Continue through the farm, over the cattle grid, and TL up the hill (opposite a much wider path signed no cycles). Where the track splits, go SO.

4 TL at TJ, back onto the road. Cycle through Troutbeck village.

5 TR at TJ, SP Windermere (6.5km/4 miles). Cycle down the hill and over the bridge in front of Limefitt Park reception.

6 Continue towards the site shop and TL just in front of it – the path goes up the hill to the left of the shop/pub. This gravel track zig zags up through green gates.

7 TR at TJ on a bridlepath.

8 Through gate, TL onto another bridleway leading to a hard rocky climb.

9 TR at TJ, onto Garburn Road (an unsigned track). The track is flat now as you pass Dubbs Reservoir on the right.   *9.5km (6 miles)*

10 TR at TJ, no SP.

11 TR at TJ with A592, SP Troutbeck.

12 Over the bridge to TL, SP Troutbeck, and climb.   *15km (9.5 miles)*

13 TL at TJ, SP Ambleside. Pass Townend.

14 TL onto a bridlepath as the road bears right.

15 TR at TJ, at A591. The road is busy as you pass Brockhole on the left – walk your bike along the pavement if the traffic is too heavy.

16 TR on the edge of Ambleside and return to the Waterhead Car Park.   ***21.5km (13.5 miles)***

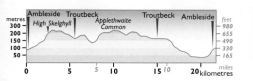

Food and drink

There are plenty of pubs and cafés in Ambleside.

Post Office, Troutbeck
Tea, coffee and cakes.

Queens Head Hotel, Troutbeck
17th-century inn serving bar meals. Outside seating.

Limefitt Park, Troutbeck
Campsite shop, passed en route.

Troutbeck village

CONISTON TO LITTLE LANGDALE, SKELWITH FORCE TO HAWKSHEAD

Route information

Distance 28km (17.5 miles)

Grade Moderate

Terrain Quiet undulating roads, except for a steep uphill section in the last quarter of the ride which takes in the beautiful views at Tarn Hows. If you wish to avoid this, simply keep to the B5285 at direction 12.

Time to allow 2–5 hours.

Getting there by car Coniston is on the A593 at the north end of Coniston Water. Park in the Coniston Car Park (pay and display) on the B5285 in the town centre.

Getting there by train There is no practical railway access to this ride.

This route is almost rectangular, with each of the four sides providing a different terrain. The route from Coniston to Langdale provides a short section of off-road along an old quarry road, from Langdale to Skelwith you will pass between the fells and then from Skelwith to Hawkshead through rolling countryside. The final section provides an opportunity to climb to one of the most beautiful views in the lakes.

Places of interest along the route

A Skelwith Force, Skelwith Bridge

One of the smaller falls in the Lake District, with a drop of around 5m (16 feet), but very attractive and with free admission. Accessible at all reasonable times.

B Hawkshead

Hawkshead was a prosperous medieval wool town. Set in the Vale of Esthwaite, the historic and picturesque village is worth spending time in – many buildings date from the 17th and 18th centuries. The village has literary connections with William Wordsworth and Beatrix Potter. The **Wordsworth Museum** is in the old Grammar School, founded by the Archbishop of York in 1585 and attended by Wordsworth between 1778 and 1787. Visitors can see the desk on which he carved his name and Anne Tyson's account book. Anne Tyson, whose house is in the village, had charge of Wordsworth while he was at the school. For further information and opening times, contact Hawkshead Tourist Information Centre on (015394) 36525. The **Beatrix Potter Gallery** is situated in the building that was once the office of her husband, solicitor William Heels, and has remained mostly unchanged since his time. Changing exhibition of Beatrix Potter's original drawings and illustrations; displays on the writer herself. National Trust property. Open March to November, Sunday-Thursday 1030–1630. Charge. Telephone (015394) 36355.

Food and drink

There are plenty of eateries in Coniston and Hawkshead.

Three Shires Inn, Little Langdale
Restaurant and bar meals, tea and coffee. Inside seating and a veranda.

Chesters Tearoom, Skelwith Bridge
Take the first left after the bridge at direction 6. Large tearoom serving snacks, soup and light lunches.

Drunken Duck Inn, near Ambleside
So called after a barrel of beer over-turned into the ducks' feed at some point during the 19th century. Restaurant and bar meals. Outdoor seating with a good view to the northeast.

Outgate Inn, Outgate
Real ale and many malts. Bar meals at lunchtime and in the evening.

Skelwith Force

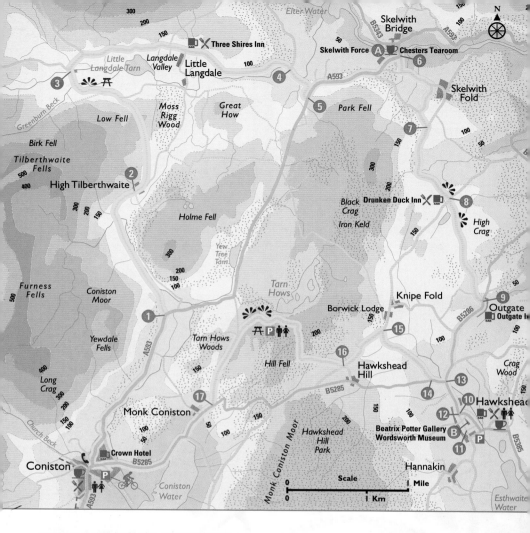

Three Shires Inn

Skelwith Bridge

Skelwith Force **A** Chesters Tearoom **6**

Elter Water

Little Langdale Tarn

Langdale Valley

Little Langdale **4**

A593

Park Fell **5**

Skelwith Fold

3

Moss Rigg Wood

Great How

7

Low Fell

Birk Fell

Tilberthwaite Fells

High Tilberthwaite **2**

Holme Fell

Black Crag

Drunken Duck Inn **8**

Iron Keld

High Crag

Yew Tree Tarn

Furness Fells

Coniston Moor

Tarn Hows

Knipe Fold

Outgate **9**

Outgate In

Borwick Lodge

15

Yewdale Fells

Tarn Hows Woods

Hill Fell

16

Hawkshead Hill

Crag Wood

Long Crag

17

B5285

13

14 **10** Hawkshead

Monk Coniston

12

Beatrix Potter Gallery
Wordsworth Museum **B**

11

Crown Hotel
B5285

Coniston

Hawkshead Hill Park

Hannakin

Coniston Water

Monk Coniston Moor

Scale

0 ——— 1 Mile

0 ——— 1 Km

Esthwaite Water

N

Route description

Leave the car park in Coniston and TL. TL at the TJ opposite the Crown hotel. Cycle through to the TJ in front of the bridge and TR along the A593 (Main Street), SP Ambleside. Continue out of Coniston.

1 TL, no SP (by the bus stop). Cycle up the hill along the single track road, briefly seeing another single track road on the right.

2 Arrive at High Tilberthwaite. Pass through the wooden gate, through the farmyard and onto the old quarry road. Continue up the track and follow the old quarry road. SO after about 1.5km (1 mile), where a footpath goes left. Descend towards the white house at bridge end. **5km (3 miles)**

3 Pass the house to your right and cross a small bridge. TR at TJ, no SP. Cycle along the Langdale valley, over a cattle grid and into Little Langdale. Continue through Little Langdale (watch out for the steep hill as you descend to the next junction).

4 TR at TJ, SP Ambleside. Climb a switch-back. ***10.5km (6.5 miles)***

5 TL at TJ onto the A593, SP Ambleside. The road is at first flat, then descends all the way towards Skelwith Bridge.

6 TR just before the bridge leading into the village, no SP. Pass the sign 'unsuitable for caravans' and start to climb. To visit Skelwith Force, go over the bridge and through the village. TL, SP Elterwater, and continue up the hill for 200m (656 feet) – the falls entrance is to the left. Retrace your route to the bridge.

7 TR at TJ, SP Hawkshead.

8 SO at XR, SP Hawkshead, by the Drunken Duck Inn. ***16km (10 miles)***

9 TR at TJ onto the B5286 (opposite the Outgate Inn). Cycle towards Hawkshead.

10 On the outskirts of Hawkshead bear left to TR into Hawkshead village. Pass Tourist Information Centre.

11 TR along Main Street. This area is part pedestrianised, so you will need to walk a short way. On the right is the Beatrix Potter gallery. ***20km (12.5 miles)***

12 Continue to TJ, TL and cycle back the way you came in.

13 TL, SP Coniston. To avoid the steep climb (but miss out on the views) stay on the B5285 and continue the route at direction 17, where SO.

14 TR, no SP. Pass a sign 'except for access' – this is the start of a fairly difficult section uphill.

15 TL at TJ, SP Coniston.

16 TR, SP Tarn Hows. Continue uphill, to the wonderful view over Tarn Hows, and then a quick descent – this is a one way road!

17 TR at TJ on B5285, SP Coniston, and return to the town. ***28km (17.5 miles)***

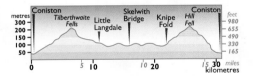

Hawkshead

Route information

 Distance   32km (20 miles)

Grade   Strenuous

Terrain   Hilly throughout – from single track fell roads early in the route to undulating minor roads through woodland. Bicycles with low gears essential.

Time to allow   3–4 hours.

Getting there by car   Kendal is on the A6. Leave the M6 at junction 36 (SP South Lakes and Kendal). Follow the signs to Kendal and then to the town centre. There are several car parks in Kendal, the most convenient being those by the river.

Getting there by train   Kendal has its own railway station but the nearest mainline station is Oxenholme, 3km (2 miles) northeast of Kendal on the B6254. Telephone (0345) 484950 for information.

This route provides contrasting scenery within a surprisingly small area – single track fell roads, rolling wooded countryside, the villages of Staveley and Underbarrow and the limestone escarpment to the west of Kendal.

Places of interest along the route

A Kendal

Kendal was the largest town in the old county of Westmorland. Sited on the River Kent, there were once over 30 mills for bobbin-making, papermaking, sawing and milling. However, Kendal was always a centre for the wool industry, which began in the 13th century. The town was granted a market charter in 1189 and a busy market is still held in the town. The **Museum of Natural History and Archaeology**, Station Road, is one of the oldest museums in the country and contains exhibits from pre-historic times through to the 20th century, on local and global archaeology, natural history, and lakeland flora and fauna. Open February to March, daily 1030–1600; April to October, daily 1030–1700; November and December, daily 1030–1600. Charge (with reduced admission to Museum of Lakeland Life and Abbot Hall). Telephone (01539) 721374. Kendal also has the **Museum of Lakeland Life and Industry**, the **Abbot Hall Art Gallery** and a ruined **castle**, once the home of Katherine Parr (Henry VIII's sixth wife). Telephone the Tourist Information Centre on (01539) 725758 for details.

B Staveley

The village of Staveley contains the **Woodcraft Workshop**. The workshop complex houses cabinet makers and skilled craftspeople pro-ducing beautiful furniture, bowls, lamps and much more. Open all year, Monday–Friday 0900–1700; Saturday and Bank Holidays 1000–1600. Also Wilf's Café and Wheelbase, south Cumbria's largest cycle shop. One of Staveley's churches is curious – the church building and tower are separated by the main street because the original benefactors could not agree on their location.

Food and drink

Kendal contains plenty of pubs, teashops and restaurants. There are also several pubs and cafés in Staveley.

Sun Inn, Crook
Bar meals available.

The Punchbowl, Underbarrow
A traditional English pub dating back to 1500. Real ales and food served all day.

River Kent, Kendal

Lakeland fells

Route description

Leave Kendal on the A6, northwards towards Shap, passing shopping complex on the right.

1 TL shortly after the shopping complex, SP Shap Road Industrial Estate/Burneside. Continue through the estate, following SP for Burneside.

2 TR just before Burneside (ruined hall to left), SP Long Sleddale, and continue along road. **6.5km (4 miles)**

3 TL at TJ (after small group of houses and telephone box). Climb to the summit of the short, steep hill, where there is a bench.

4 TL (no SP) at summit (immediately before the 6'6" restriction sign). Continue past Potter Fell and Gilpin Bank taking care on the long descent. **9.5km (6 miles)**

5 TR at TJ, SP Staveley and follow undulating road to Staveley. **17km (10.5 miles)**

6 TL at weir and war memorial. TL at TJ with main street and TL again to visit the Woodcraft Workshop. Otherwise, continue over small bridge into Station Road and cycle out of Staveley.

7 SO at bridge over A591 and on to Crook.

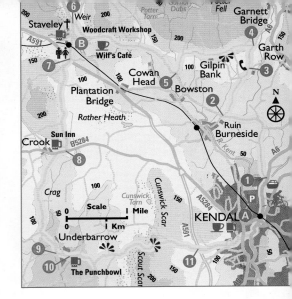

8 In Crook, TR at TJ onto the B5284, SP Bowness. Then almost immediately TL (just before the Sun Inn), to Underbarrow via Beckside. **21km (13 miles)**

9 Shortly after Underbarrow sign, LHF through village.

10 TL at TJ (opposite Punchbowl Inn) towards Kendal (25km/15.5 miles). The views make the long, steep climb ahead worthwhile.

11 Descend from Scout Scar over the A591. Continue into Kendal and the end of the route. **32km (20 miles)**

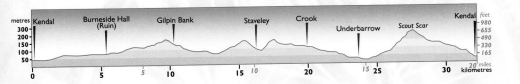

KIRKBY STEPHEN AND WESTMORLAND VILLAGES

Route information

🚲 **Distance** 37km (23 miles)

🚲 **Grade** Moderate

🚲 **Terrain** Undulating moorland roads requiring low gears.

🚲 **Time to allow** 3–4 hours.

Getting there by car Kirkby Stephen is on the A685 (from junction 38 of the M6). There is free parking in the town centre and in a signposted car park.

Getting there by train Kirkby Stephen is on the Settle–Carlisle line. Telephone (0345) 484950 for information.

This route provides a contrast with the more strenuous Lakeland rides. It goes through typical Pennine country: hilly terrain, roads often unfenced and exposed but usually less severe in gradient.

Places of interest along the route

A Kirkby Stephen

Kirkby Stephen was first settled by the Vikings. The Church of St Stephen, built in 1220, has a 16th-century tower, elegant nave and old stones. The 8th-century Loki Stone, one of only two in Europe, has a carving of Loki (a Norse god), showing him as a devil-like figure with horns. There has been a market in Kirkby Stephen since 1351 and the Cloisters, between the church and market place, were once the site of the Butter Market. For further information, contact the Kirkby Stephen Tourist Information Centre on (017683) 71199.

B Pendragon Castle

Legend says that the ruined Pendragon Castle was once the home of Uther Pendragon, father of King Arthur in the 6th century. However, castles of that time would have been constructed from wood and Pendragon Castle

Pennine country

was actually built by William Rufus some time after 1092. The castle was burned twice by the Scots, the second time in 1660. The castle was restored by Lady Anne Clifford (whose family inherited it in 1268), who stayed in it for Christmas 1663 – the first time a Clifford had stayed in the castle for over 100 years. Contact the Tourist Information Centre at Kirkby Stephen on (017683) 71199 for further information.

ⓒ Ravonstonedale

The village sits on the edge of the Howgill Fells, in limestone country. The Church of St Oswald was built in 1738 and is one of the few Georgian churches in Cumbria. There was once a refuge bell here, in a separate bell tower – any fugitive who could reach Ravonstonedale and ring the bell was free from arrest.

Food and drink

Kirkby Stephen has a host of cafés and pubs serving food for most of the day. However, by mutual agreement, the pubs are usually closed between 1400 and 1700 on Sunday.

The Bull, Nateby
Real ales and bar meals.

The Lamb Inn, near Ravonstonedale
Pub serving coffee, lunch and dinner.

Black Swan Hotel, Ravonstonedale
Full meals and bar snacks served.

The King's Head, Coldbeck
Bar meals available.

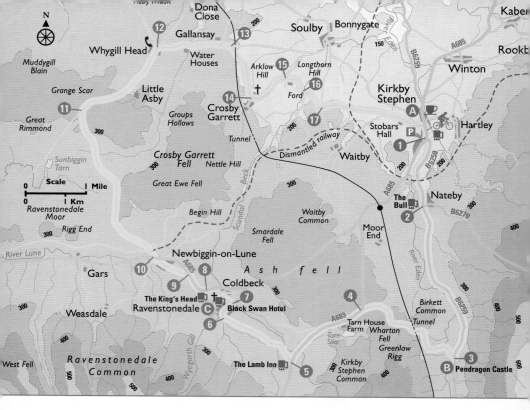

Route description

In Kirby Stephen, ride south down the main road towards Kendal.

1 TL onto the B6259, SP Hawes and Nateby and continue to Nateby.

2 SO in Nateby, towards Garsdale and Hawes, until you arrive at Pendragon Castle.

3 TR at Pendragon Castle, onto a single track road SP Ravenstonedale (7.5km/5 miles). Continue over moor, traversing Settle–Carlisle Railway which is in a tunnel here.

4 TL at TJ onto A683, past tarn and Tarn House Farm to the Lamb Inn.

5 TR at Lamb Inn, SP Ravenstonedale and continue towards Ravenstonedale.

17km (10.5 miles)

6 TR in village.

7 TL before the church (Black Swan Hotel on left) and continue to Coldbeck.

8 TL at TJ onto A685 for approximately 0.5km (0.3 mile) – take care as the road is very busy.

9 TL into Newbiggin-on-Lune. Continue through village to meet A685.

10 At TJ cross over A685, SP Kelleth and Ashby. Keep to RHF, up hill (SP Great Ashby) and out onto splendid open moorland road, bounded by snow posts on the left.

11 TR at TJ. Pass north of Little Ashby.

12 TR at XR (by telephone box), SP Soulby and Kirkby Stephen. *27km (17 miles)*

Pendragon Castle

13 TR (immediately before railway) and under railway bridge, on to Crosby Garrett, a typical Westmorland village.

14 TL in the centre of the village, SP Soulby and Kirby Stephen (31.5km/19.5 miles). Cycle past the church and out of the village, and continue for approximately 1.5km (1 mile).

15 As the road bends to the left, TR onto minor road, no SP and barn on the right. This road looks like a farm track, with grass growing down the middle. Continue down a short hill to a stream, ford and bridge.

16 SO across ford/footbridge (take care – the ford may be slippery). Continue to TJ where TL.

17 SO at XR and up hill past Stobars Hall, on to Kirby Stephen and the end of the route.

37km (23 miles)

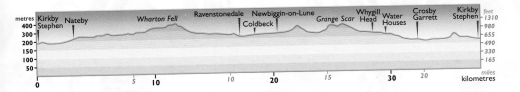

APPLEBY AND MAULDS MEABURN

Route information

Distance 43km (27 miles)

Grade Strenuous

Terrain Quiet single track lanes, narrow and hedged and across open moorland.

Time to allow 3–5 hours.

Getting there by car Appleby is just off the A66 Penrith to Brough road. Enter Appleby on the B6542 and park in the centre of town or in the long stay car park behind the church.

Getting there by train Appleby has its own railway station. Telephone (0345) 484950 for information.

This route provides plenty of contrasts. Climbing from Appleby for great views east to the Dufton Fells, the route then descends into a scenic valley containing the pretty village of Maulds Meaburn. From there a steady climb to open moorland and the fells surrounding Orton, before crossing the windswept Tarn Moor and descending to Appleby past a waterfall.

Places of interest along the route

A Appleby Castle, Appleby

This Norman castle is surrounded by 10ha (25 acres) of parkland beside the River Eden. Eleventh century keep and spectacular views; Great Hall containing the Nanking Cargo (treasure raised from the seabed). Craft exhibition, rare breed farm animals, birds and waterfowl, gardens and woodland walks. Special events held throughout the year. Tearoom and picnic area. Open March to September, daily 1000–1700; October 1000–1600. Charge. Telephone (017683) 51402.

B Great Asby Scar

National Nature Reserve run by English Nature. Great Asby Scar is an extensive area (349ha/864 acres) of limestone pavement (now a rare sight after being plundered for use in garden rockeries). Limestone bedrock was laid down over 350 million years ago. Glacial scouring during the last Ice Age left areas of the limestone open to the elements and weathering has created deep fissures and gutter-like features in the stone. Specialised flora, fauna and wild birds. Access at all reasonable times. Telephone (017683) 52347 for further information.

C Rutter Falls, near Great Asby

A wide rather than high waterfall, best viewed from the footbridge over the ford. Has a marvellously eccentric tearoom. Also Rutter Mill Gallery which exhibits contemporary arts and crafts. Open Easter to November, daily 1000–1700. Closed some Tuesdays off-season. Charge. Telephone (017683) 53243.

View of the fells from above Orton

Food and drink

There is a variety of pubs and eateries in Appleby.

The White Horse Inn, King's Meaburn
On the outward route, at the end of the village.

Butchers Arms, Crosby Ravensworth
Village pub dating from the early 1700s.

New Village Tearooms, Orton
Morning coffee, lunches and afternoon teas. Evening meals by arrangement. Garden.

Stores and Post Office, Orton
Groceries and freshly-made sandwiches.

Kennedy's Fine Chocolates, Orton
Almost 70 varieties of chocolates hand-made on the premises.

George Hotel, Orton
Real ales, lunches and evening meals. Also B&B. Garden and free camping.

The Three Greyhounds, Great Asby

Rutter Falls Tearoom
Should not be missed – an eccentric host, duck feeding and the waterfall make this a great stop. Specialist meals can be ordered in advance.

Route description

Starting at the Tourist Information Centre on Boroughgate, cycle up the hill, bear right past the castle entrance and descend to TR into Colby Lane. Continue to Colby.

1 TL, SP King's Meaburn. Climb three short sharp hills on a single track hedged lane.

2 TR at TJ, SP King's Meaburn and continue downhill. *6.5km (4 miles)*

3 To visit King's Meaburn, SO at this junction for 1km (0.6 mile). Otherwise, sharp TL, SP Maulds Meaburn and cycle through the flat grassy valley.

4 Over a bridge and TL at TJ, SP Maulds Meaburn (11km/7 miles). Pass through the pretty villages of Maulds Meaburn and Crosby Ravensworth before crossing a cattle grid onto open moorland and a climb.

5 TR at TJ, SP Orton, for a fast descent into the village. *19km (12 miles)*

6 TR, SP Orton.

7 TL at TJ (next to the tearoom and opposite the shop), no SP.

8 TR at TJ, by the George Hotel.

9 TL, SP Gaisgill and Raisbeck. Climb and then descend.

10 TL at the second road after the phone box, SP Asby (25km/15.5 miles). Cycle across the wide open moorland, past Sunbiggin Tarn.

11 TL at XR, SP Great Asby.

12 To visit Great Asby Scar, TL at XR. Cycle through village and on to nature reserve. To continue route TR at XR, SP Appleby. Cycle the undulating lane, passing the entrance to Rutter Falls on your left. *36km (22.5 miles)*

13 TL at TJ, SP Appleby.

14 TR at TJ onto the B6260, SP Appleby. *41km (25.5 miles)*

15 Descend into Appleby, past the castle to the end of the route. *43km (27 miles)*

Maulds Meaburn

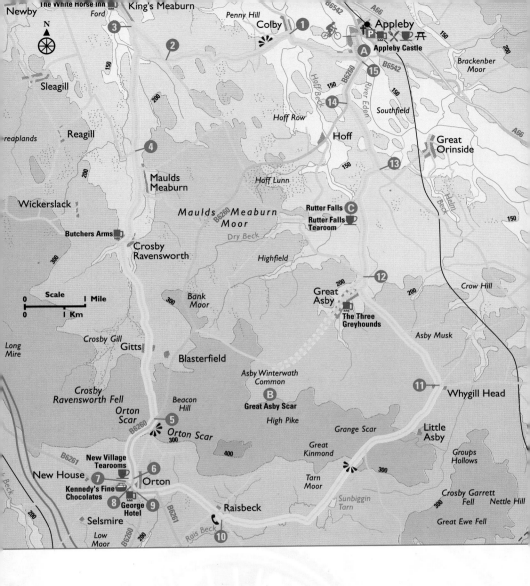

Newby

N

King's Meaburn

The White Horse Inn

Ford

3

Penny Hill

Colby

1

Appleby

P

Appleby Castle

A

15

2

Sleagill

150

200

14

B6260

Hoff Beck

River Eden

150

Southfield

Brackenber Moor

150

200

A66

reaplands

Reagill

4

Maulds Meaburn

Hoff Row

Hoff

150

Great Orinside

A66

Wickerslack

Maulds Meaburn Moor

B6260

Hoff Lunn

Rutter Falls

C

Rutter Falls Tearoom

Helm Beck

150

Butchers Arms

300

Crosby Ravensworth

Dry Beck

Highfield

Great Asby

12

200

Crow Hill

200

Scale   Mile

0

0   1 Km

Crosby Gill

Bank Moor

300

The Three Greyhounds

Asby Musk

Long Mire

Gitts

Blasterfield

Asby Winterwath Common

Whygill Head

11

Crosby Ravensworth Fell

Orton Scar

Beacon Hill

5

B6260

Orton Scar

300

Great Asby Scar

B

High Pike

Grange Scar

Great Kinmond

Little Asby

Groups Hollows

B6261

New Village Tearooms

6

New House

7

Orton

Kennedy's Fine Chocolates

8

George Hotel

9

B6261

Raisbeck

Tarn Moor

Sunbiggin Tarn

300

Crosby Garrett Fell

Nettle Hill

Selsmire

Low Moor

200

B6260

Rais Beck

10

Great Ewe Fell

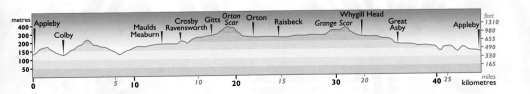

metres
400
300
200
150
100
50

Appleby

Colby

Maulds Meaburn

Crosby Ravensworth

Gitts

Orton Scar

Orton

Raisbeck

Grange Scar

Whygill Head

Great Asby

Appleby

feet
1310
980
655
490
330
165

0   5   10   20   15   30   20   40   25   kilometres
                 10   20   30   miles

EGREMONT TO ENNERDALE BRIDGE

Route information

Distance 45km (28 miles)

Grade Moderate

Terrain Quiet narrow lanes, an undulating, and sometimes steep ride across moorland, and a final trip along a car-free cyclepath makes this a ride suitable for most types of bicycle.

Time to allow 3–5 hours.

Getting there by car Egremont is on the A595 Whitehaven to Barrow-in-Furness road. Parking is available off the main street.

Getting there by train St Bees, on the West Coast Line, is the nearest railway station. You could start and finish the route from the station here, in which case TR out of St Bees station, through St Bees and go SO at direction 1.

Starting from Egremont, this route heads west to the coast and then follows a quiet narrow lane as it hugs the coastline. Then you head north to Ennerdale, along an unfenced road with panoramic views. Picking up the start of the West Cumbria cyclepath, cycle the old railway for 7.5km (5 miles) before continuing on another cyclepath back to Egremont.

Places of interest along the route

A Egremont

Egremont has a long history, reaching back to when, in 990 AD, the Danes built themselves a fort on what would later be the site of **Egremont Castle**. Devasted by the Scots in 1315 and again by Robert the Bruce in 1322, an uneasy peace followed, eventually ending in 1463 when King Edward IV made a truce with the Scots. By the beginning of the 19th century, Egremont was a thriving town with mills (producing corn, sail cloth, flint and flax) built along the River Ehen. Mining was also a major industry in the area, although only one small mine is still in operation today. Construction of Egremont Castle probably started circa 1120, although the entrance tower and courtyard are not thought to have been completed until 1180 and the Great Hall until 1270. The castle fell into disrepair in the 1400s and is now a ruin. Access at all reasonable times. Admission free. **Florence Mine** is the last deep iron mine in Europe. Heritage Centre and underground tours (suitable footwear and old clothes advised). Coffee and souvenir shop. Open March to October, daily 1000–1600. Underground tours March to June and September to October, weekends and Bank Holidays at 1030 and 1330; daily during July and August. The annual Crab Fair, dating back to 1267, is held every year on the third Saturday of September. There are field and track events, pipe smoking contests and the World Gurning Championships – the winner is the person who makes (or gurns) the most ridiculous expression.

B West Cumbria Cyclepath

The cyclepath follows an old mineral railway line, abandoned in the 1940s. The original railway was built in the 1850s to provide transportation for, and in response to the exploitation of the area's mineral resources of coal, iron ore and limestone. Lying undisturbed since the 1940s, the cyclepath has become rich in wildlife and is something of a wildlife corridor between the fells of the Lake District and Whitehaven.

St Bees

Route description

From the Tourist Information Centre on Main Street, cycle down towards the war memorial and TR into Greendykes. Take the second right towards St Bees. Continue along this road until a steep descent into St Bees.

1 TL at TJ, no SP.

2 TR, SP Nethertown (5.5km/3.5 miles). The road is narrow but little used. Pass through Nethertown and bear left in Braystones to Beckermet.

3 TL at TJ, no SP, then immediately TR, no SP. Pass the school on the right.

4 Arrive roundabout on A595. Take the second exit, SP Haile. **14.5km (9 miles)**

5 TR, no SP, just after Haile village sign.

6 TL at TJ, SP Ennerdale Bridge, and climb. To the right are the fells and the scree slopes of Wastwater. Descend towards Ennerdale. Ennerdale Water is off to the right.

7 TR at TJ, SP Ennerdale Bridge.
29.5km (18.5 miles)

8 TL into Ennerdale village, no SP. Pass the church and pub.

9 TL at TJ, no SP, towards Kirkland.

10 Arrive Kirkland. TL at XR, SP Frizington.
32km (20 miles)

11 TL, no SP, by Lamplugh school.

12 Look for the wooden arch on the right. Pass through this to begin the Ennerdale to Whitehaven section of the West Cumbrian cyclepath. Follow the signs for Whitehaven.

13 The exit from the cyclepath is tricky – passing a metal sculpture of a pig on a pole warns you that the exit is approaching. The next three trail markers are close together. Take the third trail on the left, SP Moor Row (in red). Then TL again, onto the Egremont cyclepath and follow this south to Egremont.
41.5km (26 miles)

14 The track arrives at road. TL onto road then TR at TJ, SP Bigrigg. TL, SP Egremont, cycle up then down a hill and back onto the cyclepath. Take the LHF uphill. TR at the tarmacked road TJ. SO at the roundabout, into the town centre, to end the ride.
45km (28 miles)

Food and drink

There are plenty of eateries in Egremont. St Bees has a shop and three pubs.

The Tourists, Nethertown
On the coastal section of the route.

Fox and Hounds, Ennerdale
Opposite the church. Tea and coffee available.

Shepherds Arms Hotel, Ennerdale
Hotel and bar, serving lunches and evening meals.

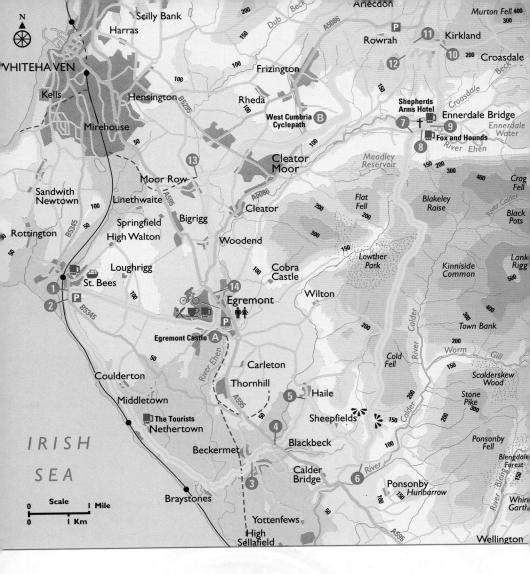

Murter Fell 400
300

Scilly Bank
Harras
200
150
100
WHITEHAVEN
Kells
Hensington
Mirehouse
50
Sandwith
Newtown
Rottington
100
50
B5345
Moor Row
Linethwaite
Springfield
High Walton
Loughrigg
St. Bees
P
Coulderton
Middletown
The Tourists
Nethertown
Beckermet
Braystones

Frizington
Rheda
West Cumbria
Cyclepath
B
100
B5595
Cleator
Moor
A5086
Cleator
Bigrigg
Woodend
Cobra
Castle
100
A595
Egremont
P
Egremont Castle
A
Carleton
Thornhill
A595
50
5
Haile
Sheepfields
4
Blackbeck
3
Calder
Bridge
Yottenfews
High
Sellafield

IRISH
SEA

Rowrah
P
12
13

Kirkland
11
10
200
Croasdale
Croasdale Beck
Shepherds
Arms Hotel
7
Ennerdale Bridge
9
Ennerdale
Water
Fox and Hounds
8
River Ehen
Meadley
Reservoir
150
200
300
400
Crag
Fell
Black
Pots
Flat
Fell
Blakeley
Raise
200
Lowther
Park
180
Kinniside
Common
Lank
Rigg
500
Wilton
Calder
River Calder
Town Bank
200
Worm Gill
Cold
Fell
150
Scalderskew
Wood
200
Stone
Pike
300
Ponsonby
Fell
Blengdale
Forest
6
River
Ponsonby
Hurlbarrow
Wellington
Whin
Garth

Scale
0   1 Mile
0   1 Km

55

GRANGE-OVER-SANDS TO HAVERTHWAITE

Route information

Distance 40km (25 miles)

Grade Moderate

Terrain Mostly minor roads, with some steep inclines. Low gears essential.

Time to allow 3–4 hours.

Getting there by car Grange-over-Sands is about 5km (3 miles) from the A590 (leave the M6 at junction 36). There is car parking in Grange in the main street (pay and display) and just beyond the railway station. Parking is sometimes difficult in Grange itself and an alternative would be Kents Bank Station car park (see below).

Getting there by train There are railway stations at Grange-over-Sands and Kents Bank. Telephone (0345) 484950 for information. To join the route from Kents Bank, leave the station and ride southwest up a long hill past Abbot Hall on the left and a post office on the right. TL at TJ with B5277. Cycle into Allithwaite and start the route at direction 2.

The route begins on the coastal plain of Grange-over-Sands and Flookburgh, continues to Cartmel and then works its way through the hills to Bigland, Haverthwaite and Newby Bridge. The return journey from Newby Bridge follows minor roads back to Cartmel and then on to Grange.

Places of interest along the route

A Holker Hall and Gardens
Stately home and beautiful award-winning 10ha (25 acre) gardens with rare plants, trees and shrubs, water features and the largest slate sundial in the world. Also Lakeland Motor Museum, Timeless Toys and Teddies Exhibition, and Bird of Prey Centre. Adventure playground, café and gift shop. Open March to October, Sunday–Friday 1030–1630. Charge. Telephone (015395) 58328.

B Lakeside and Haverthwaite Railway
Steam locomotives work this last Furness Railway branch line. Originally this line carried freight and passengers between Ulverston and Lakeside, but today it is open for 5.5km (3.5 miles) from Haverthwaite, through Newby Bridge, to Lakeside. Restaurant and tearoom.

Open daily Easter, May to November and weekends in April. Charge. Telephone (015395) 31594 for timetable information. The train service connects in Lakeside with **Windermere Lake Cruises** who run regular sailings on three ex-railway steamers between Lakeside, Bowness and Ambleside. Telephone (015395) 31188 for information. Also at Lakeside is the **Aquatarium** which takes the visitor on a voyage of exploration along a Lake District river, from its mountain top origins to Morecambe Bay. Gift shop and restaurant. Open all year, daily 0900–1700. Charge. Telephone (015395) 30153.

Lakeside and Haverthwaite Railway

Food and drink

Grange-over-Sands has many cafés, restaurants and pubs. The Coffee Pot Eating House is conveniently placed at the start and end of the route. Cartmel has several pubs and cafés (mostly situated in the main square), as does Newby Bridge.

The Engine, Cark
Pub serving bar snacks.

Rose and Crown, Cark
Bar meals available.

Newby Bridge

Route description

Start this route at the car park in Grange's main street.

1 TL onto the B5277 and cycle up the hill into and through Allithwaite. ***4km (2.5 miles)***

2 TL, SP Holy Well and Humphrey Head, on this minor road, over railway crossing.

3 TR at TJ.

4 TL at TJ onto B5278 and into Flookburgh (7.5km/5 miles). Continue on B5278 through Cark and keep left until the Rose and Crown pub.

5 TR and TL (keeping to road) at TJ towards Cartmel, and continue to Cartmel. For optional off-road route TR and TL off-road (immediately after the reverse side of the Cark-in-Cartmel road sign). Pass Rossthwaite Farm and TR at TJ (with Cumbrian Cycleway signs) onto race-course. TR into Cartmel village square where TL and join the main route at direction 8.

6 TL, SP Cartmel Priory and arrive in Cartmel village square (12km/7.5 miles). Leave the square past the stone archway.

7 RHF (LHF is to the racecourse). Pass racecourse and begin to climb.

8 LHF past Garret House, Beck Side. A series of steep climbs is ahead. Follow SP Haverthwaite.

9 LHF down steep hill (with care).

18km (11 miles)

10 Keep left and continue through wood to TJ with B5278.

11 TR onto B5278, SP Ulverston (20km/ 12.5 miles), over the bridge and on to Haverthwaite, where keep left.

12 At XR with A590, TR to visit Haverthwaite Railway Station. Otherwise SO towards Bouth and Hawkshead.

13 TR at TJ, SP Finsthwaite and Rusland.

21.5km (13.5 miles)

14 TR, SP Finsthwaite, and climb to Hill Top.

15 SO at XR towards Newby Bridge, past railway halt.

16 TR at TJ to Newby Bridge, past the Swan Hotel.

17 TL at TJ with A590 (with care). Take first right, SP Canny Hill (25.5km/16 miles). Follow road for approximately 2.5km (1.5 miles), keeping right until sharp LHF (RHF is SP No Through Road).

18 TL at TJ (no SP).

19 TR at TJ, no SP (30km/18.5 miles). Head towards Field Broughton Church (church with spire) and Cartmel.

20 Arrive Cartmel. TL, SP Grange, and climb.

36km (22.5 miles)

21 To return to Kents Bank Station, RHF, down the hill, TR at TJ and climb towards

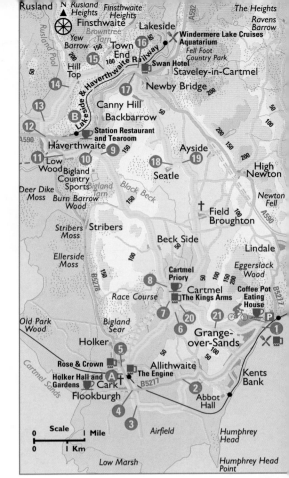

Allithwaite until SP Kents Bank Station where TL. Otherwise, LHF over Grange Fell. Follow SP to Golf Course and Town Centre, to return to the start of the route.

40km (25 miles)

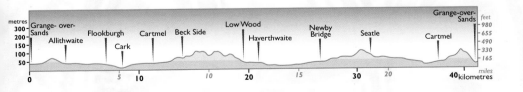

CALDBECK AND THE LAND 'BACK O' SKIDDA'

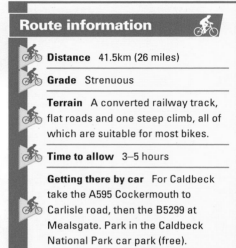

Route information

Distance 41.5km (26 miles)

Grade Strenuous

Terrain A converted railway track, flat roads and one steep climb, all of which are suitable for most bikes.

Time to allow 3–5 hours

Getting there by car For Caldbeck take the A595 Cockermouth to Carlisle road, then the B5299 at Mealsgate. Park in the Caldbeck National Park car park (free).

Getting there by train There is no practical railway access to this ride.

From Caldbeck, around the 'Back O' Skidda' past picturesque hill farms on the edge of the fells. The 'Back O' Skidda' describes the area north of Skiddaw, a mountain 6km (3.5 miles) north of Keswick. There are two sections of off-road to Bassenthwaite, before ascending to wonderful views over the Solway Firth. Through Torpenhow and Ireby and then a beautiful ride over Caldbeck Common to complete the circuit.

Places of interest along the route

A Priests Mill, Caldbeck

A watermill, built by the rector of Caldbeck on the riverbank just below the church. Used as a corn-mill between 1702 and 1933, and as a sawmill and workshop until 1965. Restored in 1986, the only machinery remaining is the 4m (14 feet) wide waterwheel, in working order. Museum, vegetarian restaurant, workshops, bookshop and bric-à-brac shop. Shops and museum open March to October, Tuesday–Sunday and Bank Holidays 1100–1700; November and December, weekends only 1100–1700. Telephone (016974) 78369. Restaurant open March to January, Tuesday–Sunday 1000–1700.

Food and drink

Old Smithy Tearoom, Caldbeck
Open Thursday–Monday for tea, coffee and snacks.

Oddfellows Arms, Caldbeck
Bar and restaurant meals served at lunchtime and in the evening.

Kirkland Stores and Post Office
Traditional village store, open every day.

The Swan Inn, Bassenthwaite
Jennings ale sold here. Bar meals served in the beamed interior.

Sun Inn, Torpenhow
William Youngers beer.

Sun Inn, Ireby
Beer and bar meals.

Paddy's Bar and Village Shop
Oak panelled bar for coffee or a guinness. Also village shop.

Bassenthwaite Lake

Caldbeck

Route description

TR out of Caldbeck car park, SP Uldale. Cycle uphill to the TJ where TR, SP Uldale.

1 TL Just past the school, no SP, and continue uphill.

2 TR at TJ, SP Fellside. Climb a very steep hill.

3 TL, SP Fellside. Cycle past the hill farms away from all the traffic.

4 As the road bends to the right, TL over the bridge with white metal fencing either side and dead end sign (at 5.5km/3.5 miles). Cycle over Uldale Common along a reasonable track — where the track splits take LHF (which is effectively SO).

5 TL, no SP, at the road junction. Continue over a bridge and up a steep hill.

6 At XR of roads and bridleway, TR SP Public Bridleway, Bassenthwaite, and through gate into a pasture (the road to the left goes towards Skiddaw House). To help route finding here, large white dots have been painted along the way – follow them! As you pass from the road and through the gate, head in a 10 o'clock direction to a gate in the corner, through which is a signed XR of bridleways. SO here, SP Bassenthwaite Village. Follow the fence on your left through three gates, arriving at the corner of a field. TR for 100 metres then TL through a gate and follow the line of old tree stumps down to the village.

7 TR at TJ, no SP. Pass Green Farm and cycle through Bassenthwaite, with the Swan Inn on your left. As you leave the village, watch out for the seat (on the left) with its great view of Bassenthwaite Lake. ***15km (9.5 miles)***

8 TR at TJ, no SP. Then TR, SP Uldale.

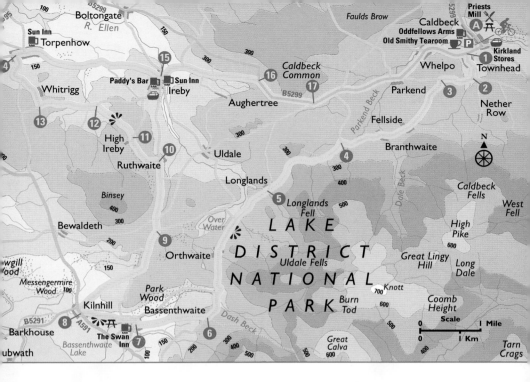

9 TL, SP Ireby. **20km (12.5 miles)**

10 TL, SP High Ireby.

11 Cycle through High Ireby and TL, no SP. NB: do not take the turn next to Manor Farm, take the next one 50 metres later, once you have left the village. Pass sheep pens on the left as you cycle the track. Marvellous views of the Solway Firth open up in front.

12 TL at TJ, no SP. Enter Whitrigg.

13 TR, SP Torpenhow. **25.5km (16 miles)**

14 TR at TJ, SP Ireby.

15 SO at XR in Ireby, SP Caldbeck (if you want a pub or shop TR at this point). **32km (20 miles)**

16 TR at TJ, SP Caldbeck. Cycle along the B5299 and onto Caldbeck Common. **34.5km (21.5 miles)**

17 TL at TJ, SP Caldbeck and return to the start of the route. Arrive back into Caldbeck. **41.5km (26 miles)**

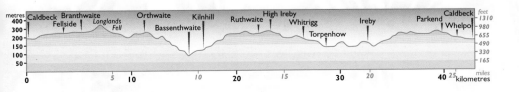

WESTERN LAKELAND – BROUGHTON TO ESKDALE GREEN

Route information

Distance 44km (27.5 miles)

Grade Strenuous

Terrain This route involves a large amount of climbing – some of the climbs are especially steep and a bike with low gears is essential.

Time to allow 3–4 hours.

Getting there by car Broughton in Furness is 48km (30 miles) west of the M6, junction 36, on the A593. There is free car parking by the town square in the centre of Broughton.

Getting there by train Foxfield, 2.5km (1.5 miles) south of Broughton, has a railway station on the Barrow/West Coast line. Telephone (0345) 484950 for information.

This ride takes in some spectacular mountain scenery, especially between Dunnerdale and Eskdale. Mostly on remote minor roads, the route traverses three separate uplands: the Dunnerdale Fells, Birker Fell and Corney Fell. Most of the roads are relatively free from traffic, although the final 16km (10 miles) back to Broughton, designated by the tourist board as a Scenic Route, can have a surprising number of cars at certain times of the day. Note that much of this ride is in remote areas – cyclists should ensure they are properly prepared and take some food and drink with them.

View from Muncaster Castle

Places of interest along the route

These are mostly outstanding views of the Lake District:

A Dunnerdale Fells
Before the descent of Kiln Bank, between directions 2 and 3. A splendid view of Coniston Fells and down into Dunnerdale.

B Birker Fell

Between directions 4 and 5, near SP Stockley Beck. Stunning panoramic views of the western Lakeland skyline.

C Muncaster Castle, Ravenglass

Muncaster Castle has been inhabited since 1208 and visitors can see antique furniture, paintings and silverware, and the haunted Tapestry Room. Also woodland gardens containing rare and exotic plants and the Owl Centre, headquarters of the World Owl Trust and the site of one of the finest collections of owls in the world. An informative talk and display is given at the Owl Centre March to November, daily 1430. Plant centre, gift shop and café. Castle open March to November, Sunday–Friday 1230–1600. Gardens and Owl Centre open all year, daily 1100–1700. Charge. Telephone (01229) 717614.

D Corney Fell

From Corney Fell between directions 7 and 8 – a view seawards of the east coastline of the Isle of Man and its highest point, Snaefell. Ahead the sombre lines of Black Combe.

E Prior Park

Descending towards direction 8 – another view of Coniston Fells and, to the right in the far distance, the wind generators on the fells above Lowick.

Route description

Leave the square in Broughton on the A593, SP Torver and Coniston, heading northeast for approximately 2.5km (1.5 miles).

1 TL, SP Broughton Mills, for a climb and then descent into Broughton Mills.

2 LHF at telephone kiosk, over bridge and RHF, SP Seathwaite and Duddon Valley (4.5km/3 miles). Continue the long, steep climb over Dunnerdale Fells and cycle down Kiln Bank (taking care on the descent) to Hall Dunnerdale.

3 TL at TJ (10km/6 miles), SP Broughton via Duddon Valley, and cycle down the valley.

4 TR, SP Eskdale and Whitehaven. There is now a steep climb (initially 1:4) up Birker Fell – the road takes on all the characteristics of a remote mountain road. Devoke Water, the Lake District's most remote lake, is out of sight but can be visited by TL SP Woodend Farm and following the bridleway for a short while. Retrace your route to the road to continue the ride. Take care on the steep descent towards Eskdale.

5 TL SP Birkby Road (approximately 1.5km (1 mile) before Eskdale Green), and follow minor road by south bank of the River Esk.
20.5km (12.5 miles)

6 To visit Muncaster Castle, TR at TJ onto A595. To continue route, TL at TJ onto A595, SP Barrow. Climb steep hill. *26.5km (16.5 miles)*

7 Near the summit of the hill, TL SP Corney and Broughton Scenic Route (29km/18 miles). Continue to climb Corney Fell. After summit of hill, continue on road SP Broughton.

8 Take LHF.

9 RHF then very steep descent through woods to the Duddon valley.

10 TL at Duddon Bridge TJ towards Broughton, onto the A595. *42km (26 miles)*

11 TL onto A593 then TR into Broughton and the end of the route. *45km (28 miles)*

Food and drink

Broughton in Furness has a number of pubs which serve meals and bar snacks, an Italian restaurant called 42 The Square and the Broughton Bakery and Tearooms.

Blacksmith's Arms, Broughton Mills
Bar meals served 1200–1400 and 1800–2100.

Post Office and Store, Ulpha
Approximately 0.5km (0.3 mile) outside the village.

King George IV, Eskdale Green
Bar meals and lunches. This is slightly off the main route but the only chance of a meal at the halfway point. At direction 5 continue right for 1.5km (1 mile) into Eskdale Green.

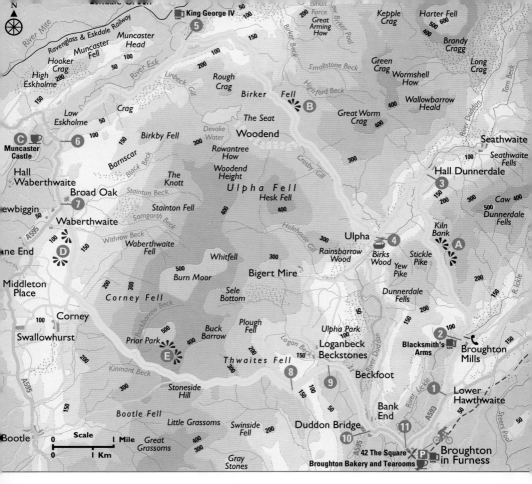

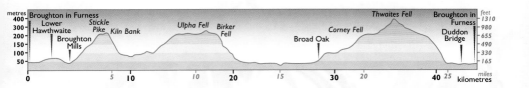

CONISTON WATER AND GRIZEDALE FOREST

Route information

Distance 45km (28 miles)

Grade Strenuous

Terrain A series of minor roads, many single track with very steep inclines, and 7.5km (5 miles) of off-road riding along forest tracks. Low gears essential. On the off-road section bicycles with narrow section tyres may be at a disadvantage to those with broader tyres/off-road cycles.

Time to allow 3–4 hours.

Getting there by car Coniston is on the A593 and can be reached from the M6, junction 35. There is ample car parking in Coniston – a convenient pay and display car park is off the B5285 Hawkshead road.

Getting there by train There is no practical railway access to this ride.

This route climbs out from Coniston to the top of the ridge separating Coniston and Hawkshead. At High Cross the road is abandoned in favour of 7.5km (5 miles) of way-marked forest tracks through Grizedale Forest. The route then follows a series of narrow roads eventually crossing over the fells to the southeast of Coniston Water. The final 12.5km (8 miles) provide a splendid, gradually unfolding panorama of the Coniston range. There are further forest trails between Grizedale and Satterthwaite – a detailed plan of the trails can be obtained from Grizedale Visitor Centre.

Places of interest along the route

A Coniston

The village of Coniston sits at the top of Coniston Water and became popular as a tourist resort in the 1800s. The Victorian philosopher, critic and artist John Ruskin lived at nearby Brantwood and is buried in St Andrews Churchyard. Arthur Ransome based much of his book, *Swallows and Amazons* on Coniston Water, which was also the scene of Donald Campbell's world water speed record in his boat *Bluebird*. Coniston grew during the 19th century when over 500 people were involved in local copper and slate mining. In 1859 a railway was built and the railway company also launched their steam yacht, *Gondola*. Now fully restored by the the National Trust, *Gondola* makes regular sailings on Coniston Water from March to October, daily. Charge. Telephone (015394) 41288 for times of sailings. Also providing trips on Coniston Water is *Coniston Launch*, which has special interest cruises including Campbells on Coniston, Conservation, and Swallow and Amazons. Open mid March to mid November and over Christmas. Charge. Telephone (015394) 36216 for information.

B Grizedale Forest Park

Famous for its forest sculptures, Grizedale Forest Park was first managed in the 11th century by the monks of Furness Abbey. There is an extensive range of waymarked trails, an adventure playground and picnic areas. Visitor centre with shop, tearoom and forest exhibition in Grizedale. Open March to October, daily

1000–1700; November to February, Monday–Friday 1000–1600, weekends 1000–1700. Telephone (01229) 860010.

 Brantwood, Coniston

Brantwood was the home of John Ruskin between 1872 and 1900. Situated right on the shore of Coniston Water, the house is beautifully situated with marvellous views of the surrounding mountains. Visitors can see a large collection of Ruskin's drawings and paintings. Also craft and picture gallery, and bookshop. Coffee house/restaurant next door. Open March to November, daily 1100–1730; December to February, Wednesday–Sunday 1100–1600. Telephone (015394) 41396.

Coniston

Route description

TL out of the car park onto the B5285.

1 Stay on the B5285, through Monk Coniston and climb up through the woods to High Cross.

2 TR onto the waymarked forest track (4km/2.5 miles). The forest tracks are way-marked by green posts with a cycle logo and, initially, red direction arrows. Follow the track for approximately 3km (2 miles).

3 Then take RHF, following posts with blue direction arrows to Grizedale.

4 TR onto road and cycle through Satterthwaite.

5 TL onto minor road, SP Dale Park and Hawkshead.

6 TR at TJ, SP Rusland Cross.

7 TL and follow SP towards Haverthwaite.
20km (12.5 miles)

8 At junction almost within sight of the main road (A590), TR to Bouth.
25km (15.5 miles)

9 TR at White Hart Inn and continue on a

Coniston Water from Brantwood

series of single track roads following SP to Oxen Park.

10 SO at TJ, no SP, towards Bandrake and Lowick Bridge. Take care – steep descent.

11 TR at TJ (32.5km/20 miles), then continue past Nibthwaite Grange and High Nibthwaite. Follow east shore of Coniston Water, passing Brantwood on the right.

12 1.5km (1 mile) past Brantwood, TL.

13 TL at TJ onto B5285 and return to Coniston and the end of the route.

45km (28 miles)

Food and drink

Coniston has plenty of cafés and pubs and there is a café at Grizedale Visitor Centre.

Eagle's Head, Satterthwaite
Good food and real ale.

White Hart Inn, Booth
Bar meals available.

Jumping Jenny Coffee House and Restaurant
Licensed restaurant situated next door to Ruskin's home.

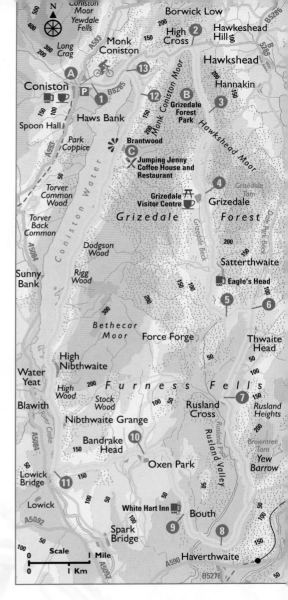

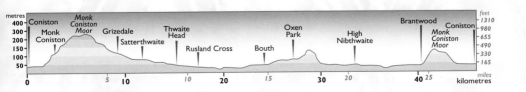

WHINLATTER AND HONISTER PASSES

Route information

Distance 45km (28 miles)

Grade Strenuous

Terrain This route takes in two steep passes – Honister is by far the steeper with the first half mile being especially tough. Aside from these, the terrain is undulating and the surface is excellent.

Time to allow 3–6 hours.

Getting there by car Grange is just off the B5289 Keswick to Cockermouth road. Parking is difficult in the village and you may find that you need to use the car parks in Rosthwaite or Seatoller villages further down the Borrowdale valley.

Getting there by train There is no practical railway access to this ride.

A tough route from Grange, through Honister Pass, past Buttermere and Crummock Water to High Lorton, then through the Whinlatter Pass and back to Grange. Borrowdale is usually busy, but beyond it the roads are very quiet. The west side of Derwent Water is a treat, missed by most, and gives an unusual view of the lake.

Places of interest along the route

A The Bowder Stone

A large isolated rock, in a state of delicate balance. The Bowder Stone weighs around 1,930,400kg (1900 tons) and a ladder allows you to climb to the top. Access at all reasonable times. Admission free.

Grange

Food and drink

There are two tearooms in Grange. Lorton has a post office/stores and the general store at Braithwaite also holds a small selection of bicycle spares.

Flock Inn Tearoom, Rosthwaite
Tearoom and a village shop.

The Yew Tree, Seatoller
Restaurant serving light lunches and teas.

Croft House Café, Buttermere
Mugs of tea and coffee, as well as snacks and ice cream.

Bridge Hotel, Buttermere
Morning coffee, bar lunches and afternoon tea.

The Fish Hotel, Buttermere

Swinside Inn, Swinside
Extensive and tasty menu.

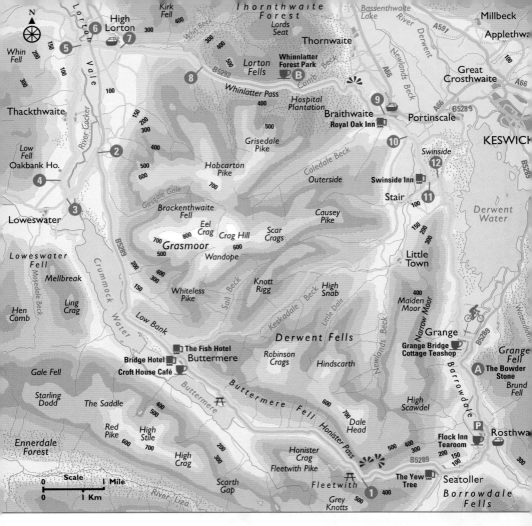

B Whinnlatter Forest Park

England's only mountain forest is situated at the summit of Whinlatter Pass, about 305m (1000 feet) above sea level. Badger set, forest trail, conservation trail, waymarked mountain routes and orienteering. Also Exhibition Centre, with audio visual presentation telling the story of the forest, and various interactive displays. Shop and tearoom. Operated by Forest Enterprise. Open all year, daily (except 2 weeks in January – telephone for further information). Telephone (017687) 78469.

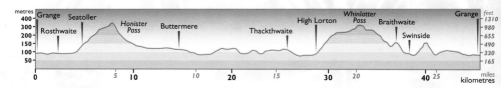

Route description

Leave Grange over the double bridges and TR onto the B5289, following SP Rosthwaite. The entrance to the Bowder Stone is 1km (0.6 mile) on your left. Stay on the B5289 and pass through Rosthwaite and Seatoller.

1 Begin a very steep climb up to Honister Pass and continue alongside the river to Buttermere Lake and then Buttermere village. Still on the B5289, follow the eastern edge of Crummock Water.

2 TL at TJ, SP Scale Hill.

21.5km (13.5 miles)

3 TR, SP Thackthwaite.

4 TR at TJ, no SP (24km/15 miles). Pass Oakbank House on your left and cycle through Thackthwaite.

5 TR at TJ, over the bridge SP Cockermouth.

6 TR at the staggered XR, then TL SP Keswick. Pass the Post Office/stores.

7 TR, SP Boon Beck and Scales – take care not to miss this turn. Start a long climb.

29km (18 miles)

8 TR onto the B5292, towards Keswick. The entrance to Whinlatter Forest Park is at the top of the hill. Descend the hill into Braithwaite, with a grand view of Bassenthwaite Lake.

9 In Braithwaite, TR next to the Royal Oak Inn. Follow the signs (three altogether!) to Newlands.

10 TL, SP Swinside.

11 TL at the TJ next to the Swinside Inn, SP Portinscale. *39.5km (24.5 miles)*

12 TR at the large triangular junction, then TL at the TJ, SP Grange. Climb to the top of the switchback and freewheel to the edge of Grange and the end of the route.

45km (28 miles)

Honister Pass

Route 18
MARYPORT – CUMBRIAN COAST AND COUNTRYSIDE

Route information

Distance 59.5km (37 miles)

Grade Easy

Terrain Mostly flat terrain along B roads

Time to allow 3–5 hours.

Getting there by car Maryport is on the A596 Workington to Carlisle road. Park on South Quay (free), by the sea and close to the Tourist Information Centre.

Getting there by train There is a railway station at Maryport. Telephone (0345) 484950 for information.

Starting in Maryport, the route heads north along the coast for views across the Solway Firth. The sea breezes should help you along. Passing through the seaside resorts of Allonby and Silloth, the route turns inland to return through the pretty villages of Abbeytown and Westnewton. There are plenty of good opportunities for picnics along the coast, particularly Allonby and Silloth promenade.

Places of interest along the route

Ⓐ Maryport

Traces of Bronze Age settlements have been discovered in Maryport. The Romans built a fort just to the north of the present town, which became a key feature in Hadrian's Wall.

Senhouse Roman Museum, the Battery, Sea Brows, contains a large collection of Roman artefacts, started in the 1570s by John Senhouse. Open April to June, October and Bank Holidays, Tuesday and Thursday–Sunday 1000–1700; July to September, daily 1000–1700; November to March, Friday–Sunday 1030–1600. Charge. Telephone (01900) 816168. The modern town of Maryport was founded in 1749 by an Act of Parliament sponsored by Humphrey Senhouse II. He named the town after his wife, Mary. The port itself was built to support the coal trade, but other industries followed, making Maryport for a time the largest port in Cumberland. **Maryport Maritime Museum**, Senhouse Street, tells the story of the town and its maritime history through fascinating objects, pictures, models and paintings. Open April to October, Monday–Thursday 1000–1700, Friday and Saturday 1000–1300 and 1400–1700, Sunday 1400–1700; November to March, Monday–Saturday 1000–1300 and 1400–1630. Admission free. Telephone (01900) 813738. Elizabeth Dock in Maryport contains two steamships that are open to visitors. The *Flying Buzzard*, built in 1951 and now restored, was a steam tug of the Clyde Shipping Company. Guided tours take the visitor around the wheelhouse, crew's quarters, engine and boiler room. The *VIC96* was built as a naval supply ship during World War II and still has the original coal-fired steam engine, in working condition. An exhibition in the ship's hold lets visitors raise and lower sails, tie ship's knots and try a sailor's hammock. Open April to October, daily 1000–1600; November to March, tours by arrangement. Charge. Telephone (01900) 815954. **Maryport Aquaria**, South Quay, contains over 30 creative displays, letting you explore the secrets of the underwater world. Gift shop and café. Open all year, daily 1000–1700. Charge. Telephone (01900) 817760.

Ⓑ Crosscanonby Saltpans

There are the remains of saltpans here, between the road and the shoreline. These works were probably constructed circa 1650 and appear to have closed in 1736. The salt was produced by filtering water through the sand in a large circular structure, lined with clay. The resulting brine was boiled to remove impurities and then slowly heated to produce salt crystals. Wooden structures revealed by the tide are the remains of a pump and water tank scaffold. Access at all reasonable times.

Ⓒ Silloth

Silloth was a Victorian seaside resort, overlooking the Solway Firth and the hills of south Scotland. It is known for its invigorating air and beautiful sunsets. The town retains its broad, tree-lined and cobbled main street, a large green and an attractive promenade.

Ⓓ Abbeytown

Abbeytown grew up around the Abbey of Holm Cultram, founded in 1150. The abbey was sacked by Robert the Bruce in 1319 and today survives as the parish church of St Mary (it was the only building in the village strong enough to survive the attack of Scottish raiders). Abbeytown is one of the most attractive villages in the area.

Maryport Harbour

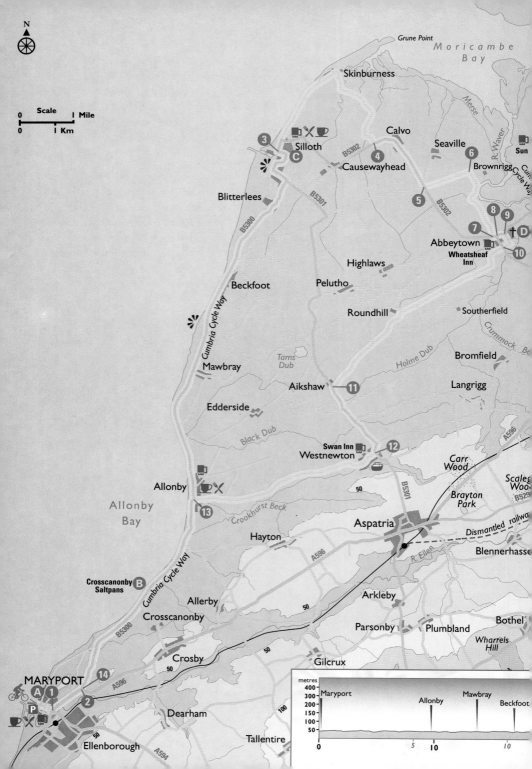

Route description

Start from the Tourist Information Centre on Senhouse Street. Cycle up the hill and TL into High Street, SP All Through Traffic. To visit Senhouse Roman Museum, continue to the end of the High Street, TL into Solway Terrace and follow this road through the bollards to the Museum. Otherwise, TR from the High Street into Wood Street, SP All Through Traffic.

1 TL at the traffic lights, SP Carlisle A596.

2 TL onto the B5300, SP Allonby. This road runs parallel to the coast all the way to Silloth, giving numerous opportunities for stopping to picnic or paddle. Pass through the seaside town of Allonby and the smaller Mawbray and continue into Silloth.

3 In Silloth, TR into Griffel Street and cycle parallel to the sea front, following the signs for Skinburness (21.5km/13.5 miles). Pass through Skinburness and TR sharply in front of the hotel.

4 TL at TJ, SP Abbeytown.

5 TL at XR, SP Brownrigg. *30.5km (19 miles)*

6 TR at TJ, SP Abbeytown.

7 TL at TJ in Abbeytown, SP Wigton.

8 TL, SP Newton Arlosh.

9 TR opposite Holm Coltran Abbey, SP Wigton, and go round a right hand bend.
35.5km (22 miles)

Food and drink

Maryport has numerous places for refreshment, as do Allonby and Silloth, typical seaside resorts. There is a convenience store in Westnewton.

Wheatsheaf Inn, Abbeytown
In one of the area's most attractive villages.

Swan Inn, Westnewton
Freehouse serving home cooked meals. Accommodation, garaging for bicycles, garden and play area.

10 SO at XR, SP Southerfield. Continue to TJ with B5301.

11 TL at TJ onto the B5301, SP Westnewton. *42.5km (26.5 miles)*

12 TR, SP Allonby, and go through the pretty village of Westnewton.

13 Arrive Allonby and TL at TJ onto the B5300, SP Maryport. *51.5km (32 miles)*

14 TR at TJ onto the A596, SP Maryport (57km/35.5 miles). TR at XR, TL into High Street and then TR into Senhouse Street to the end of the route. *59.5km (37 miles)*

EASTERN LAKELAND FELLS – KIRKBY LONSDALE TO SEDBERGH

Route information

 Distance 58km (36 miles)

Grade Strenuous

Terrain Undulating moorland roads early in the route contrast with typical dales terrain after Sedbergh. Mostly steady climbs, apart from one, Barbondale. There is an optional route which avoids this hard climb, adding 5.5km (3.5 miles) to the total distance.

Time to allow 4–5 hours.

 Getting there by car Kirkby Lonsdale lies to the north of the A65 Skipton to Kendal road – easily accessible from the M6, junction 36, and via the main roads from Kendal and Barrow. There is ample car parking in two pay and display car parks on New Road, and there is free parking near Devil's Bridge (A683 Sedbergh road).

Getting there by train There is no practical railway access to this ride.

This route brings together the uplands bounding the River Lune and the Howegills (far eastern Lakeland fells), and the western edge of the Yorkshire Dales. It is a ride full of interest and contrast, and links the three historical towns of Kirkby Lonsdale, Sedbergh and Dent.

Places of interest along the route

Ⓐ Kirkby Lonsdale
Kirkby Lonsdale is a traditional market town with market square and 600-year-old cross, situated on the banks of the River Lune. The main street and its surrounds are worth exploring. Turner painted the view from the churchyard of the Lune Valley and Ruskin described it as 'one of the loveliest scenes in England'. Nearby Devil's Bridge, on the return route, is thought to be at least 600 years old. There is a working blacksmith on the left as you leave the town.

Ⓑ Fox's Pulpit
George Fox (1624–91) was the English founder of the Quaker Society. The son of a puritan weaver, he preached all over the country, advocating a simple way of life and worship. His sincere and captivating oratory inspired thousands of people from all over the north of England to convert. He preached at this spot on Sunday, 13 June 1652 and a plaque on the rock commemorates the event.

Ⓒ Sedbergh
Surrounded by fells, Sedbergh is an old market town with cobbled streets. There has been a community here for hundreds of years. St Andrews church, originally Norman, has examples of every period of ecclesiastical architecture since then. Just outside Sedbergh

River Dee, Dentdale

is **Brigflatts**, the oldest complete Meeting House still in use, with an original oak interior. Open all year, daily. Services held Sundays, 1030. Telephone (015396) 20125.

Ⓓ Dent

Dent is a beautiful Dales village, with cobbled main street, and a memorial fountain commemorating Professor Adam Sedgwick (1785–1853) who was Professor of Geology at Cambridge and born in Dent. **Dent Craft Centre** is situated in a converted hay barn. There was a print workshop here at one time and a Victorian printing press, in working order, can be seen. There are resident craftspeople at the centre and visitors can see pottery, candle making, metal work and original oil and watercolour painting. Restaurant and B&B. Telephone to confirm opening times on (015396) 25400.

Food and drink

Kirkby Lonsdale, Sedbergh and Dent all have a number of cafés and pubs.

Posthorn Café, Sedbergh
On the left as you enter the town – favoured by local cyclists.

Dent Craft Centre, 3km (2 miles) before Dent
Coffee, tea and snacks.

The Head, Middleton
Bar snacks.

Devil's Bridge, Kirkby Lonsdale
There is a caravan here selling hot food, sandwiches, cakes and drinks.

N

Birchfield

Swarth Greaves
Great Dummacks
Brant Fell
Arant Haw
Nab

Lambrigg Fell

Docker Fell

9

Firbank Fell

Fox's Pulpit
B

Firbank

R. Lune

37

8
7
New Field

Posthorn Café

Sedbergh
Downbiggin

13
C
14

Lily Mere

10

Grassrigg

12
A683
Brigflatts Friends Meeting House

Millthrop

Frastow Fells

West Mosta

Killington Reservoir

6

Holme Farm

11

Holme Fell
Holme Knott

Helmside

Bendrigg

Old Park

Killington

Beckside

Brown Knott

Dent Craft Centre

Bendrigg Lodge

Harprigg

Raismoor

Cartsaddle Hill

Gawthrop

15
D
Den

Stone Close Café
Meadowside Café

5
4

Park Hill

3

The Head

Middleton

Middleton Fell

Weather Ling Hill

Calf Top

Towns Fell

Wyndhammere

Kitmere

Rigmaden Park

R. Lune

Applegarth

Howegill Head

Crag Side

Crag Hill

Warth Hill

Kitridding Hill

Blease Hill

Showrigg Hill

Ashdale Gill

Barbon High Fell

Tarnhouse Tarn

2

Old Town

Mansergh

Thorn Moor

Barbon

Barbon Beck

Barkin Beck

Barbondale

Terrybank Tarn

Deansbiggin

16

Barbon Low Fell

Fowlstone

A65

Kearstwick

Casterton

17

Brownthwaite

Ease Gill

Scale
1 Mile
1 Km

Hutton Roof

Moor End

A
1
Kirkby Lonsdale
P

18

High Casterton

19
Devil's Bridge

B6254

P

metres
400
300
200
150
100
50

Kirkby Lonsdale
Kearstwick
Old Town
Killingto
Bendrigg

0
5
10
10

82

Route description

Leave Kirkby Lonsdale on the B6254 (New Road) following one-way system up the hill. TR, SP Old Town and Old Hutton, and descend hill.

1 TL, SP Old Town and Old Hutton, and cycle up hill, past blacksmiths on left and Kirkby Lonsdale Rugby Football Club on the right, and continue out of the town.

2 TR by milestone at Old Town, SP Killington and Sedbergh. *5km (3 miles)*

3 TL, SP Old Hutton and Kendal.

4 LHF, SP Old Hutton and Kendal. *10km (6 miles)*

5 TR, by small plantation, and follow road to east of M6 past Bendrigg Lodge and Killington Reservoir (several Reservoir SP en route).

6 TL at TJ at end of reservoir. *16km (10 miles)*

7 TL at TJ onto A684, SP Kendal.

8 TR, SP Lambrigg and Beckfoot, and follow road to the east of the M6, towards Tebay Gorge.

9 As road bears left, TR onto single track road (wooden SP BirchField) and pass Fox's Pulpit on the left between two cattle grids. Continue towards Sedbergh, down steep hill.

10 SO at XR with A684, onto B6256, SP Middleton and Kirkby Lonsdale for approximately 1.5km (1 mile)

11 TL immediately after Yorkshire Dales National Park plaque, no SP, following single track road. Take RHF.

12 TL at TJ onto A683, to Sedbergh. Pass Briggflatts Friends Meeting House on the right.

13 TR at TJ with A684, into Sedbergh. Continue through Sedbergh leaving town on road SP Dent. *31.5km (19.5 miles)*

14 Continue on this road – it follows the north bank of the River Dee, eventually passing Dent Craft Centre on the left.

15 Continue into Dent or TR, SP Barbon Gawthrop. For optional route avoiding the very steep climb of Barbondale, TR again and head north west, along a minor road to the south of the River Dee. Keep left (eventually on minor gated road with grass growing in middle) until Holme Farm. TL at farm then TL at TJ onto A683. TL immediately after the Head pub at Middleton, onto minor road. Then TR and follow minor road down valley and through Barbon village. TL onto A683 to rejoin route at direction 18, where continue on A683.

Otherwise, to tackle the main route and its climb, continue SO. The climb is in two sections – the initial 1:5 levels out for a short way before becoming a 1:7. Then descend to a beck.

16 TL at TJ, SP Casterton and Kirkby Lonsdale. *50km (31 miles)*

17 TR at XR, onto narrow lane.

18 TL at TJ with A683, towards Casterton – take care here, particularly from traffic approaching from the right (54.5km/34 miles). Continue through Casterton.

19 Arrive at Devils Bridge and continue on to Kirkby Lonsdale and the end of the route. *58km (36 miles)*

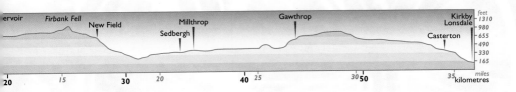

Route 20

LAKE WINDERMERE AND CONISTON WATER

Route information

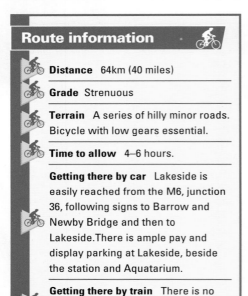

Distance 64km (40 miles)

Grade Strenuous

Terrain A series of hilly minor roads. Bicycle with low gears essential.

Time to allow 4–6 hours.

Getting there by car Lakeside is easily reached from the M6, junction 36, following signs to Barrow and Newby Bridge and then to Lakeside. There is ample pay and display parking at Lakeside, beside the station and Aquatarium.

Getting there by train There is no practical railway access to this ride.

Taking in both Lake Windermere and Coniston Water, the route starts along the west side of Lake Windermere, skirting Esthwaite Water en route to Hawkshead and Brathay. After following part of the Langdale Valley, the route cuts through to Coniston Water, with a short diversion to visit one of the Lake District's most photographed beauty spots – Tarn Hows. Then along the east side of Coniston Water before cutting over the fells separating the two major valleys.

Throughout the ride there are spectacular views across Lake Windermere, of the Langdales and of the Coniston range. On a good day this is one of the finest rides in the southern Lake District.

Places of interest along the route

A Lakeside

The **Lakeside and Haverthwaite Railway** runs steam trains on the remaining 5.5km (3.5 miles) of the original Furness Railway branch line, from Lakeside, through Newby Bridge to Haverthwaite. Café at Lakeside Station. Open daily, Easter and May to November, also weekends in April. Telephone (015395) 31594 for timetable information. The trains connect with **Windermere Lake Cruises** who run regular steamer sailings throughout the year. Telephone (015395) 31188. **Lakeside Aquatarium** describes the journey of a Lakeland river, from mountain top to Morecambe Bay. Gift shop, restaurant and café. Open all year, daily 0900–1700. Charge. Telephone (015395) 30153.

B Stott Park Bobbin Mill

This is a working heritage museum – one of the best preserved genuine early 19th-century working mills. A guided tour describes the story of the cotton mill, wooden bobbin manufacturing and the people who worked here. Exhibition and woodland picnic area. Operated by English Heritage. Open March to October, daily 1000–1800 (or dusk if earlier). Steam engine operation Tuesday–Thursday. Charge. Telephone (015395) 31087.

C Hill Top Farm

Hill Top Farm was Beatrix Potter's home and was where she wrote many Peter Rabbit books. The 17th-century cottage contains her furniture and china. The cottage is small and the number of visitors limited to a maximum of 800 per day – long queues are likely during busy periods.

National Trust property. Lunch and evening bar meals available at National Trust owned pub, the Tower Bank Arms, next door. Cottage open Good Friday and March to October, Saturday–Wednesday 1100–1700. Charge. Telephone (015394) 36269.

Ⓓ Tarn Hows

Tarns are small mountain lakes or pools (from an old Norse word). Tarn Hows is one of the most visited places in the Lake District, with one of the best views – 1km (0.6 miles) long and surrounded by woods with a path all the way around. Tarn Hows is best avoided on Bank Holiday weekends and during school holidays because it gets so busy. National Trust property. Accessible at all reasonable times. Admission free. Telephone the National Trust Regional Office on (015394) 35599 for information.

Ⓔ Brantwood, Coniston

Brantwood was the home of John Ruskin between 1972 and 1900. One of the best views across the lake to the Coniston Fells can be seen from Ruskin's study. See Route 16 for further information.

Food and drink

There are refreshments available at Lakeside, and a variety of pubs and cafés in Hawkshead.

Sawrey Hotel, Far Sawrey
Bar lunches and dinners.

Tower Bank Arms, Near Sawrey
Coffees, teas and bar meals.

Drunken Duck, Skelwith Fold
Fine bar snacks, and lunch and evening meals.

White Hart Inn, Bouth
Good bar snacks.

Tarn Hows

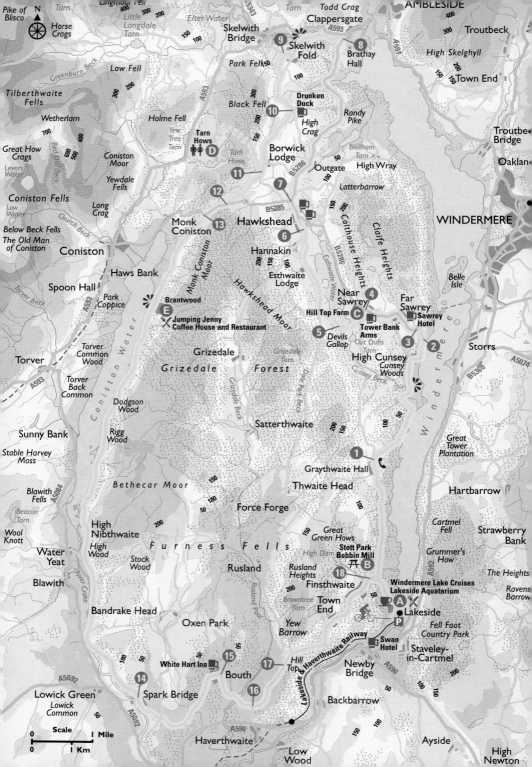

Route description

TR out of Lakeside car park and follow minor road towards Hawkshead, past Stott Park Bobbin Mill and Graythwaite Hall.

1 TR by telephone kiosk, SP Cunsey and Ferry (4km/2.5 miles). Descend steep hill through Cunsey Wood and continue through Cunsey.

2 TL at TJ, SP Windermere and Ferry. Climb hill towards Far Sawrey, ignoring right turn to ferry.

3 TL at TJ and follow signs to Hawkshead (9km/5.5 miles). Ride through Far Sawrey to Near Sawrey.

4 TL, SP Lakeside and Hawkshead Youth Hostel, past Hill Top Farm. *11km (7 miles)*

5 TR and TR again, near west bank of Esthwaite Water. Continue past Esthwaite Lodge (Hawkshead Youth Hostel) to Hawkshead.

6 TL into Hawkshead village (15.5km/9.5 miles). Ride through Hawkshead, leaving it on the B5285, SP Coniston.

7 TR onto B5286, SP Ambleside. Cycle through Outgate and on to Brathay.

8 TL at Brathay sign (immediately before bridge over Langdale Beck), SP Skelwith Fold. Follow minor road along south side of beck to Skelwith Fold. *22km (13.5 miles)*

9 TL, SP Hawkshead, and continue.

10 AT XR (by Drunken Duck) TR, SP Coniston and Tarn Hows. *26km (16 miles)*

11 TR up hill to Tarn Hows – retrace your route to the road where TR.

12 TR at TJ onto B5285, towards Monk Coniston. *32.5km (20 miles)*

13 TL, SP Brantwood, onto minor road running the full length of Coniston Water. Pass Brantwood (37km/23 miles) and continue until beyond the lake, passing through Nibthwaite to Spark Bridge.

14 LHF, keeping L through village. TL and then TR to Bouth. *50km (31 miles)*

15 Arrive Bouth. TR following SP to Newby Bridge. *53.5km (33 miles)*

16 TL, SP Finsthwaite and Rusland.

17 TR 1.5km (1 mile) further on, SP Finsthwaite, for a steep climb to Hill Top (56.5km/35 miles). Continue to Finsthwaite.

18 TR past Stott Park Bobbin Mill and back to Lakeside and the end of the route. *64km (40 miles)*

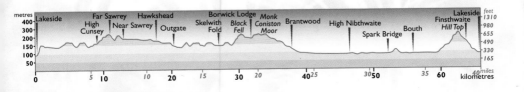

WAST WATER AND THE HARD KNOTT PASS

Route information

 Distance 65km (40.5 miles)

Grade Strenuous

Terrain This is quite a challenging ride, with two passes to be climbed and much of the rest of the route over undulating roads. However, with no sections of off-road, it makes for a good day's cycling on most types of bike.

Time to allow 4–8 hours.

Getting there by car Gosforth is just off the A595 Workington to Barrow road. There is a free car park in the centre of town.

Getting there by train The nearest railway station is at Seascale. From the station take the B5344 east. TL at TJ onto A595, then TR to Gosforth and the start of the route.

This route goes from Gosforth to Wast Water, the deepest of all the lakes. From there into Eskdale, passing the Ravenglass and Eskdale Railway and Boot. Then a climb over the Hard Knott Pass with great views and the old Roman Fort of Mediobogdum. A fast descent takes you to an undulating ride along the beautiful Duddon Valley, which inspired Wordsworth to compose a series of sonnets dedicated to the

river and vale. From here back to Eskdale, with wide views that provide a marvellous contrast to everything else on the ride so far, and then back to Gosforth.

Places of interest along the route

A Gosforth
St Mary's Churchyard contains a 4.5m (15 foot) high 11th-century Viking Cross and, in the church itself, a Chinese Bell, captured at Anunghoy Fort, on the Canton River, in 1841. Gosforth Pottery has a huge range of pots for sale and you can throw a pot yourself. Open April to September, daily 1000–1730; October to December and March, Tuesday–Saturday 1000–1700; January and February, Thursday–Sunday 1000–1700.

B Ravenglass and Eskdale Railway
The Ravenglass and Eskdale Railway, or 'La'al Ratty' as it is know locally, was opened in 1875 to carry iron ore to the Furness Railway. Now restored, the narrow gauge track runs for 11km (7 miles) between Dalegarth Station and Ravenglass. The return journey takes around two hours. Tearoom. Open all year. Charge. Telephone (01229) 717171 for details of the timetable.

C Eskdale Mill
The mill, dating from 1578, is one of the few remaining two wheel water corn mills in the country. Renovated by Cumbria County Council, much of the mill has been restored to working order. A fascinating exhibition explains the milling process and the workings of the wooden

machinery. At the rear of the mill are the waterfalls that provide the power to run the wheels. Demonstrations of the mill operating by prior arrangement only. Gift shop selling light refreshments. Open March to September, Tuesday–Sunday 1100–1700. Charge. Telephone (01946) 23335.

Mediobogdum Roman Fort
Built during Hadrian's reign (117–138AD), the fort was occupied for 50 years. It provided a central link between the forts at Ravenglass and Ambleside. The fort is located on the left hand side of Hard Knott Pass, on the uphill section. Access at all reasonable times.

Start of the Hard Knott Pass

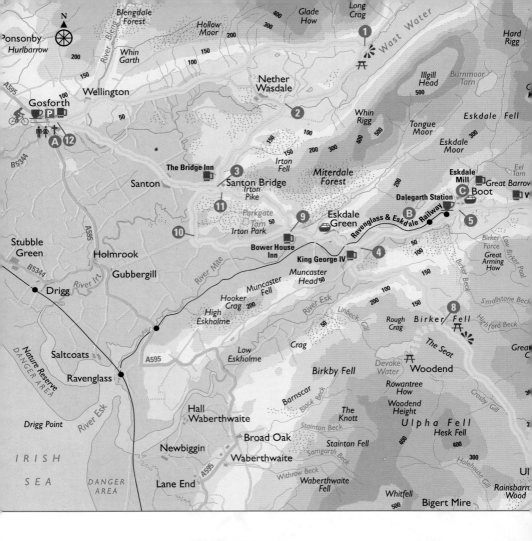

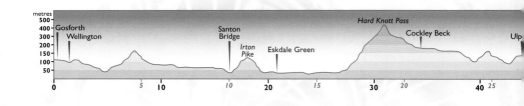

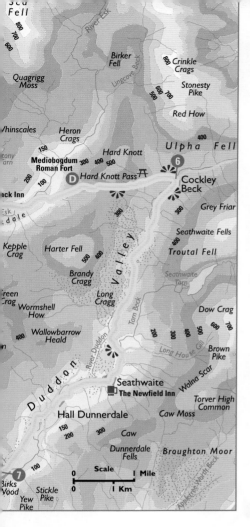

Route description

TL out of the car park, pass Midland Bank and TL, SP Wasdale. Cycle out of Gosforth up a steep hill and then a gradual climb until you swoop down to the edge of Wast Water.

1   TR at TJ, SP Wasdale.   **9.5km (6 miles)**

2   TL at TJ, SP Santon Bridge.

3   TL at TJ, SP Eskdale, and climb a steep hill. Keep left by the Bower House Inn. Continue through Eskdale Green to TJ.   **15km (9.5 miles)**

4   TL at TJ, SP Boot. Continue towards Boot.

5   To visit the Eskdale Mill and Boot, TL. Otherwise, continue along the valley, past Mediobogdum Roman Fort, for a magnificent view from the top of Hard Knott Pass and a fast descent.

6   TR at TJ, SP Broughton via Duddon Valley (32km/20 miles). Cycle the beautiful rolling road of the Duddon Valley.

7   TR, SP Eskdale, for an uphill cycle.
43km (27 miles)

8   At the sign for Stanley Gill at the top of the pass, it is worth taking the rough track opposite for a look at Devoke Water (48km/30 miles). Continuing on the main route, TL to join the outward road and go back through Eskdale Green.

9   TL just after the Bower House Inn, SP Holmrook.   **54km (33.5 miles)**

10   TR at TJ, SP Santon Bridge.
58km (36 miles)

11   TL at TJ, SP Gosforth and continue back to Gosforth.

12   Arrive back into Gosforth. The car park is on your right.   **65km (40.5 miles)**

HAWESWATER AND THE SLEDDALE VALLEY

Route information

Distance 69km (43 miles)

Grade Strenuous

Terrain Single track, walled lanes. Three off-road sections, some steep and rocky (although the compiler of this route did them on a road bike). The section along the old Roman road has few landmarks and should not be tackled in bad weather or poor visibility.

Time to allow 4–8 hours.

Getting there by car Shap is on the A6, Kendal to Penrith road. Parking is available along this road.

Getting there by train Although the railway passes through Shap, there is no station. Kendal station is the closest, from where you can reach the route on the northbound A6 at direction 6, adding 10.5km (6.5 miles) round trip to the total distance.

From Shap the route goes west along quiet lanes to the lovely Haweswater Reservoir and then over the Gatescarth Pass on a steep, rocky bridleway and through the Long Sleddale Valley. Although the views make the effort worthwhile, you may wish to avoid this strenuous part of the route and there is an alternative route that avoids the Gatescarth Pass. The route then follows a series of narrow lanes to a delightful and flat section of off-road through the Borrowdale Valley. From there north, parallel to the M6 watching the cars racing to Penrith, before a final piece of off-road on the old Roman road over Coalpit Hill and back to Shap. Although there are refreshment stops en route, much of this route is off-road and remote, and cyclists should take food and drink with them.

Places of interest along the route

A Shap Abbey

Shap Abbey was founded in 1180 and is one of the few Premonstratensian abbeys still standing – the tower and low surrounding walls have survived. Empty stone coffins in the old floor can still be seen. English Heritage property. Accessible at all reasonable times. Admission free.

B Haweswater

In 1929 the Manchester Water Corporation started the construction of a dam to raise the level of Haweswater in order to supply Manchester with water, creating Haweswater Reservoir. It is 6.5km (4 miles) long, 1km (0.6 mile) wide and 60m (198 feet) deep. The isolation and tortuous road access make Haweswater one of the quieter lakes in the area.

Haweswater

Food and drink

Shap has pubs, tearooms and shops.

Haweswater Hotel, Haweswater
Teas, coffees and meals. Wonderful outside seating with a good view of the lake. This would be a good place to turn around if you do not wish to attempt the Gatescarth Pass.

Stockdale Craft Workshop, Stockdale
Teas and coffees available.

The Cross Keys, Tebay
Bar meals available.

Crown and Mitre, Bampton Grange
On the alternative route. Food available.

Route description

From Shap, cycle north along the A6 to the end of the town. TL, SP Bampton. To visit Shap Abbey, SO as road swings right, SP Abbey, and follow the road downhill to the abbey ruins. Otherwise continue to Rosgill.

1 TL, SP Rosgill. Down quite a steep hill through the village.

2 TL, SP Haweswater.   *5.5km (3.5 miles)*

3 TL at XR, SP Haweswater. Cycle along the south shore of the reservoir, past the Haweswater Hotel to the end of the road and a car park. To take the alternative route avoiding the Gatescarth Path, turn around at the car park (or at the hotel) and cycle back alongside the reservoir.

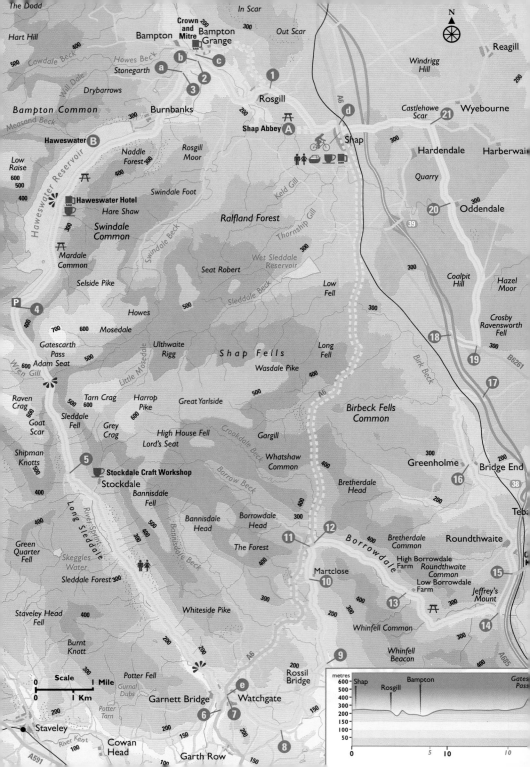

a   TR at XR, SP Bampton Grange.

b   TL at TJ, SP Bampton.

c   TR at TJ, SP Shap. Cycle over the bridge into Bampton Grange. Continue. TL at junction by Rosgill and carry on to A6 junction.

d   TR , no SP, and cycle down the A6.

e   Pick up main route at direction 7, where TL, SP Patton Bridge.

4   To continue main route, continue through gate at the end of the car park, SP MCWW public footpath (16km/10 miles). TL, SP Public Bridlepath Long Sleddale. The track is steep and difficult to cycle, but the views are fantastic. At the top pass through a gate and follow the well defined track down.

5   TL at TJ by a bridge, no SP. Cycle the Long Sleddale Valley.

6   TL at TJ, onto the A6.   **30.5km (19 miles)**

7   TR, SP Patton Bridge.

8   TL at XR, SP Rossil Bridge. Cross the bridge and cycle along an undulating hedged lane.

9   TL at TJ, no SP. Cross a cattle grid and cycle along a gated road.   **36km (22.5 miles)**

10   Pass through a gate, past a white house with a tennis court, then through another gate. As the lane goes to the left, TR through a metal gate and onto a grassy track that takes you up the right side of the valley.

11   TR at TJ onto the A6, no SP, and continue until the road swings to the left.
    40km (25 miles)

12   TR, no SP, through a metal gate and down into the valley. Cycle along the track to the right of the stream, across bridge and

through an open field with the ruins of High Borrowdale Farm on the left. Continue through the gate above Low Borrowdale farm.

13   RHF downhill, through the farm yard and out onto the farm track. Cross over two cattle grids and through the quiet scenic valley where, eventually, the tarmac surface restarts.

14   TL at TJ onto A685 (opposite two bridges carrying the railway and the M6), no SP.

15   TL, SP Roundthwaite. If you require refreshment carry on over the motorway to Tebay.

16   TL at TJ (effectively straight on), SP Shap (51km/31.5 miles). Pass under the railway and the northbound carriageway of the M6.

17   TL, SP Shap. Quite bizarre this, as it feels like you are cycling the fast lane of the motorway.   **55.5km (34.5 miles)**

18   TR at TJ, SP Orton. Warning: if it is at all misty you should not follow the route over the old Roman road (direction 19). Instead, TL here, following the road to Shap.

19   TL just after the quarry, SP Bridlepath Oddendale (59.5km/37 miles). Follow the old Roman road uphill as it passes over Coalpit Hill. Just over the top of the hill, adjacent to the cairn, the track splits three ways – take the left hand track and aim for the group of trees on the horizon. Pass a plantation to your right, between a stone circle, where the track becomes distinct again.

20   TL at TJ with tarmac road, continue uphill and skirt the edge of the quarry.
    63.5km (39.5 miles)

21   TL at TJ, no SP. Cross over the M6, back into Shap and the end of the route.
    69km (43 miles)

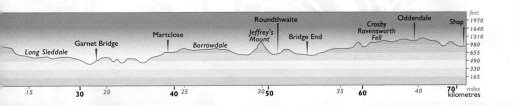

KENDAL AND LAKE WINDERMERE

Route information

Distance 77 km (48 miles)

Grade Strenuous

Terrain Mostly minor roads, but there are a number of strenuous climbs which require low gears.

Time to allow 4–6 hours.

Getting there by car Leave the M6 at junction 36, SP South Lakes and Kendal. Follow SP to Kendal and then to town centre. There are several car parks in Kendal – those by the river are the most convenient.

Getting there by train There is a branch line railway station at Kendal, but it may prove to be easier to use Oxenholme Station which is on the main Euston/Carlisle/Glasgow line. Oxenholme is only 3km (2 miles) from Kendal – use the B6254. Telephone (0345) 484950 for information.

This is a first-rate Lakeland route taking in the ridge to the west of Kendal, crossing the Lyth Valley and climbing Strawberry Bank (the pièce de résistance of the day's climbs), before descending from Gummers How to Fell Foot on the southeast shore of Lake Windermere. The route then follows the west side of the lake for most of its length, before taking in Ambleside and Troutbeck. From Troutbeck on a series of single track and gated roads, before a climb over the limestone escarpment which separates Brigsteer from Kendal.

Places of interest along the route

A Kendal
See also Route 9. The **Museum of Lakeland Life and Industry** illustrates the Lake District and its rich heritage. Open mid February to March, daily 1030–1600; April to December, daily 1030–1700. Charge. Telephone (01539) 722464. **Abbot Hall Art Gallery** contains a wide range of fine art including paintings by George Romney, Sutherland, Spencer, Turner, Ruskin and others. Opening times and telephone number as per Museum of Lakeland Life and Industry. The Friends Meeting House in Kendal dates from the early 19th century and contains the **Quaker Tapestry Exhibition** – over 50 panels of embroidery celebrating the experiences of the Quakers since 1652. Open April to October, Monday–Saturday 1000–1700. Charge. Telephone (01539) 722975. Kendal also has the **Museum of Natural History and Archaeology** and a ruined **castle**, once the home of Katherine Parr (Henry VIII's sixth wife) – see Route 9.

B Lyth Gallery, Crossthwaite
Displays of oils, watercolours, pastels and sculpture. Open all year, Wednesday–Sunday 1100–1700.

C Gummers How
A favourite viewpoint high above Lake Windermere.

D Fell Foot Park and Garden
At the extreme south end of Lake Windermere, this 7ha (17 acre) park and garden is in the process of being restored to its Victorian glory. Access to the shores of Lake Windermere. Bathing area, rowing boats for hire, children's adventure playground, woodland trail and tearoom. National Trust property. Open all year,

Food and drink

Kendal, Hawkshead and Ambleside have numerous cafés, restaurants, pubs and hotels. The Sun Inn, Crook, the Punchbowl Hotel, Underbarrow and the Wheatsheaf Inn, Brigsteer all serve bar meals.

Bowland Bridge Café, Bowland Bridge
CTC appointed café on the right as you enter the village.

Sawrey Hotel, Far Sawrey
Bar meals served.

Tower Bank Arms, Near Sawrey
Immediately after SP to Hill Top Farm. Bar snacks and meals available.

Little Chef, Ings
On the main road, to the left of the village.

daily 0900–1900 (or dusk if earlier). Charge. Telephone (015395) 31273.

Ⓔ Lakeside
At Lakeside is the **Lakeside and Haverthwaite Railway**, **Windermere Lake Cruises** and Lakeside **Aquatarium** – see Route 20.

Ⓕ Stott Park Bobbin Mill
A working heritage museum – see Route 20.

Ⓖ Hill Top Farm
Beatrix Potter's home – see Route 20.

Ⓗ Ambleside
Popular centre for climbers and walkers, Ambleside can get extremely busy during the summer. The Old Bridge House, a well-known landmark and now a National Trust shop, is a small cottage built on a packhorse bridge. **Adrian Sankey's** workshop contains a collection of traditional and contemporary lead crystal glass and visitors can see the glassware being created. Open all year, daily 0900–1730. Admission free. Telephone (015394) 33039. The

Kirkstone Galleries contain a large collection of Cumbrian crafts. Coffee shop. Open April to October, daily 1000–1800; November to March, daily 1000–1700. Admission free. Telephone (015394) 34002. The **Armitt Collection** was created by three sisters who, in 1912, founded a library to support their love of the arts and writing. Open all year, daily 1000–1700. Charge. Telephone (015394) 33949.

Route description

From the riverside car park, follow the one-way system (using left lane) through main street.

1 TL at traffic lights into Allhallows Lane (becoming Beast Bank), SP Underbarrow and Brigsteer. There follows a long steep climb out of Kendal. Cross the Kendal bypass by road bridge and continue up to summit of Scout Crag. Carry on through Underbarrow, following SP to Crosthwaite.

2 TR at TJ, past Punchbowl Hotel and church, through village. **9.5km (6 miles)**

3 TR at TJ onto A5074 Lyth Valley road, SP Winster. TL, SP Bowland Bridge, and continue to Bowland Bridge.

4 Take road towards Newby Bridge. This climb – Strawberry Bank – is very steep and continues for nearly 3km (2 miles). Pass Gummers How at the summit. Care required on steep descent. Fell Foot is to the left.

5 TL at TJ onto A592.
20km (12.5 miles)

6 Arrive Newby Bridge. TR at TJ onto A590, SP Barrow. Immediately TR again to Swan Hotel and Lakeside. Care – this is a busy road. From Lakeside (23.5km/14.5 miles) continue on minor road hugging west shore of Lake Windermere. Climb through Graythwaite.

7 TR at junction (by telephone kiosk), SP Cunsey, Sawrey and Ferry (27.5km/17 miles). Cycle through Cunsey Wood and Cunsey.

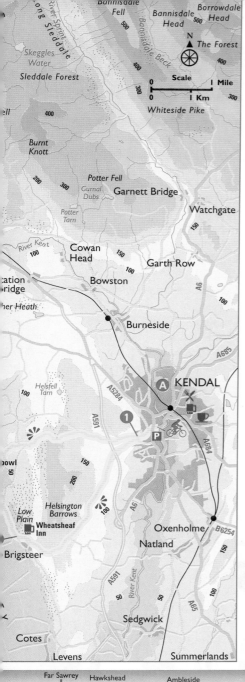

8 TL at TJ onto B5285, SP Hawkshead (32.5km/20 miles). Continue through Sawrey, passing Hill Top Farm, to Hawkshead.

9 TR at TJ onto B5286, SP Ambleside (37.5km/23.5 miles). Continue through Outgate and Brathay.

10 At Clappersgate, TR at TJ onto A593, SP Ambleside.   **43.5km (27 miles)**

11 TR to Waterhead, immediately after bridge. Take RHF (A591) towards Windermere.

12 TL immediately after Low Wood Hotel, SP Troutbeck. Continue into Troutbeck village.

13 TR at TJ onto A592, back in the direction of Windermere. Continue past The Howe.   **52km (32.5 miles)**

14 Approximately 2.5km (1.5 miles) after The Howe, TL onto minor road, no SP but opposite SP for Troutbeck. Continue towards Kentmere and Ings.

15 At TJ cross A591. Immediately after shelter on right, TR onto gated road (59km/36.5 miles). Continue under railway bridge, ensuring that you close all gates behind you.

16 TL at TJ at Borwick Fold cattle grid, no SP, and continue to Crook.

17 TL at TJ onto B5284 (immediately after Sun Inn).   **64.5km (40 miles)**

18 TR, SP Underbarrow. Continue past Beckside and into Underbarrow where keep left.

19 TR at TJ opposite Punchbowl Hotel, then immediately TL, SP Brigsteer.   **68.5km (42.5 miles)**

20 Arrive Brigsteer. Take LHF, SP Kendal (71.5km/44.5 miles). Descend towards Kendal. On entering Kendal, TR (Gillingate) and TL at TJ (Main Street), to join one-way system and return to riverside car park.   **77km (48 miles)**

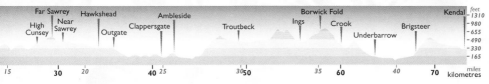

AMBLESIDE LOOP – ULLSWATER, THIRLMERE AND GRASMERE

Route information

Distance 78km (48.5 miles)

Grade Strenuous

Terrain With the paucity of roads in central lakeland, there are a number of stretches of A road in this ride – special care should be taken along the northern shore of Ullswater. This ride is ideal for the experienced cyclist looking for a challenging day.

Time to allow 5–8 hours.

Getting there by car Ambleside is on the A591 Keswick to Windermere road. Park in the Rydal Road car park on the A591 at the northern end of town.

Getting there by train There is no practical railway access to this ride.

This ride starts in Ambleside and uses a quiet minor road to climb the Kirkstone Pass where, with a backward glance, you will glimpse Lake Windermere. The route joins the A592 to swoop down to Brotherswater and on to Ullswater. Having admired Aira Force, the route goes uphill before traversing east to Dacre Castle (private home – not open to the public). Then west towards Threlkeld, mostly parallel to the A66, before passing through St John's Beck and along the shore of Thirlmere. Then past Grasmere and Rydal Water to the end of the route.

Places of interest along the route

A Aira Force

Aira Force has been a popular beauty spot for over 200 years, inspiring many poets and writers including Wordsworth and Coleridge. The impressive waterfall drops 21m (70 feet) from below a stone footbridge. In 1906 the area containing the falls was put up for sale as housing plots. The newly formed National Trust put up an appeal and raised £12,000 to purchase the 304ha (750 acre) site. Café open April to November, daily. Waterfall accessible at all reasonable times. Admission free. Telephone (015394) 35599 for information.

B Dacre

Dacre church is built on the site of a Saxon monastery. Dacre Castle has a 14th-century tower and 2m (7 feet) thick walls. The Castle is a private residence and not open to the public.

C Threlkeld Quarry and Mining Museum

There is evidence of mining in Cumbria as long ago as the 12th century. Threlkeld Museum illustrates the history, methods and heritage of local mining through hundreds of fascinating artefacts. Mineral collection and geology room. Pictorial record of Threlkeld and other Cumbrian quarries. Gift shop. Open April to October, daily 1000–1645. Charge. Telephone (017687) 79747.

D Dove Cottage, Grasmere

Dove Cottage was William Wordsworth's home

between 1799 and 1808. Guided tours available of the house and (weather permitting) the garden. Also the award-winning Wordsworth Museum displaying a unique collection of manuscripts, books and paintings interpreting the life and work of Wordsworth. Changing exhibitions. Gift shop and tearoom (serving evening meals July and August). Open all year, daily 0930–1730. Charge (discount ticket with Rydal Mount and Wordsworth House, Cockermouth — see Route 4). Telephone (015394) 35651.

Kirkstone Pass

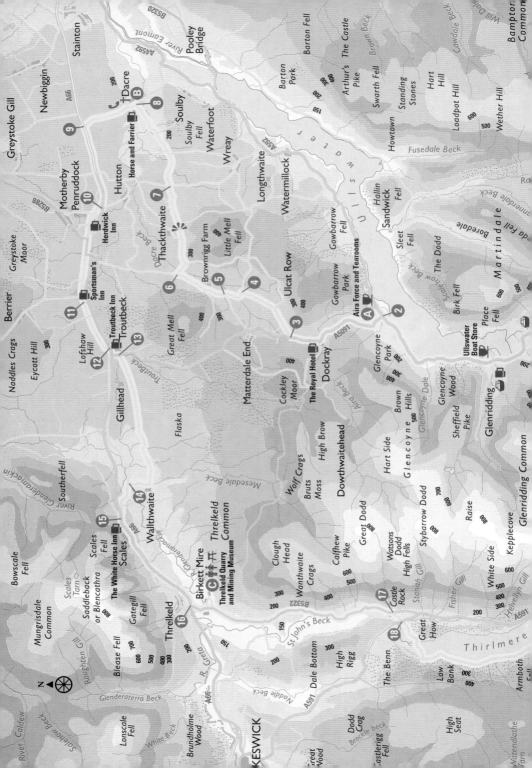

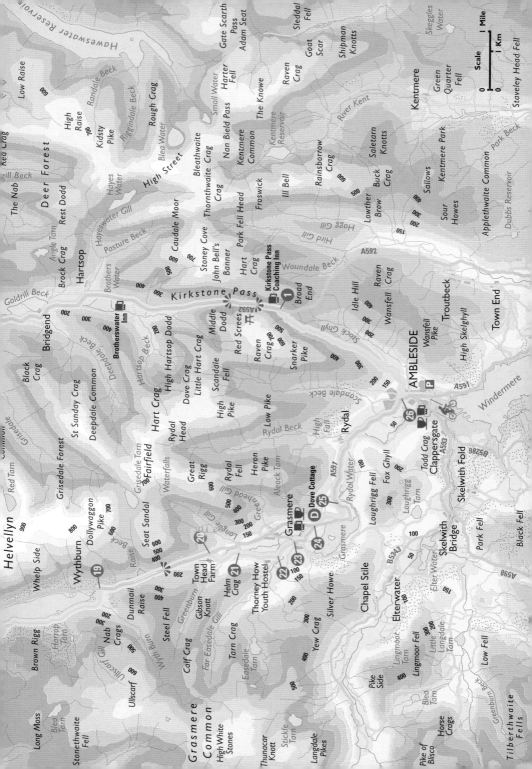

Route description

Leave the Rydal Road car park and TR onto the A591, SP Tourist Information. Take the first left along Smithy Brow, SP Kirkstone. Pass Rowenfield Country House on the right and climb towards the pass.

1 TL onto the A592, SP Patterdal (5km/3 miles), and through the Kirkstone Pass. Sweep down into Patterdale, through Glenridding and along the north shore of Ullswater.

2 Continue past the turn for the A5091. TL, SP Aira Force. After visiting the falls, return to A592 where TR. Then TR onto A5091, SP Dockray. Climb a steep hill and pass through Dockray. *19.5km (12 miles)*

3 TR, SP Penruddock.

4 TL at TJ, SP Penruddock. *24km (15 miles)*

5 TR at TJ, no SP. Pass Brownrigg Farm on the right.

6 TR, SP Thackthwaite.

7 SO at XR, SP Dacre. *30km (18.5 miles)*

8 Enter Dacre. TL at TJ, SP Penruddock. For a view of Dacre Castle, TR through metal gate (just before the red telephone box) and walk 0.5km (0.3 miles) down the track – remember it is a private residence. Continue out of Dacre and up the steep hill.

9 TL at TJ onto the A66, SP Keswick.

10 TR, SP Penruddock Pass. Continue through Penruddock. *36km (22.5 miles)*

11 TR just after the Sportsman's Inn onto the old A66 (it runs parallel to the new road)
39.5km (24.5 miles)

12 TR at TJ with A66, no SP. Then, TL, SP Dockray. Pass the Troutbeck Inn.

13 TR, SP Gillhead. Continue along a quiet narrow lane until the road bends sharply to the right.

14 TL at the TJ, no SP. *45.5km (28.5 miles)*

15 TL at TJ for a short downhill ride of the the A66, SP Keswick.

16 TL onto the B5322, SP Thirlmere. Pass the entrance to Threlkeld Mining Museum on the left and cycle along the pretty valley.
50km (31 miles)

17 This turn is easy to miss – TR just after left-hand SP for Castle Rock B&B, SP Grasmere via Permissive Cycleway.
56km (35 miles)

18 SO at XR with A591, SP Public Road Around Lake. Follow the road around the west side of Thirlmere.

19 TR at TJ, SP Grasmere. Cycle over the pass. *66km (41 miles)*

20 TR past a width restriction sign, halfway down the other side. Pass Town Head Farm on the right.

21 TR, no SP (do not cross the bridge). Pass Thorney How Youth Hostel.
70km (43.5 miles)

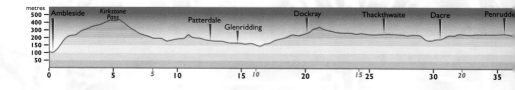

22   TL at TJ, no SP. Pass the car park.

23   SO at XR, into College Street. TL at TJ opposite Dale Lodge Hotel, no SP.

24   TR at TJ with the A591, then immediately TL, SP Dove Cottage.   ***72.5km (45 miles)***

25   TL onto A591.

26   Cycle back into Ambleside and TR into the car park.   ***78km (48.5 miles)***

Food and drink

Ambleside and Grasmere have numerous tearooms and pubs. Patterdale has a village post office and store. There is a kiosk on the lake edge at Glenridding selling tea, coffee and ice cream. Also food store and pubs in the village itself.

Kirkstone Pass Coaching Inn, Kirkstone Pass
Lakeland's highest inn with outside seating and good views.

Brotherswater Inn, Patterdale
Meals available.

The Royal Hotel, Dockray
Teas, coffees and meals.

Horse and Farrier, Dacre
Village pub.

Herdwick Inn, Penruddock
Modern and spacious pub.

Aira Force

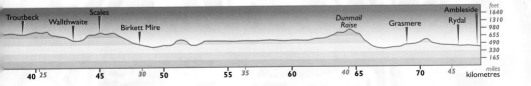

KENDAL TO ULLSWATER LOOP – A GRANDE RANDONNÉE

Route information

 Distance 109.5km (68 miles)

Grade Strenuous

Terrain This is a challenging and hilly route. Several long climbs, including Kirkstone Pass and Shap – low gears essential. An optional route, linking Long Sleddale to Haweswater Reservoir via Gatescarth Pass, is given for off-road enthusiasts, adding up to 2 hours to the riding time. Please note that the optional route is over a mountain pass – cyclists should wear suitable clothing and carry food and drink with them.

Time to allow 6–7 hours.

Getting there by car Kendal is on the A6. Leave the M6 at junction 36 and follow signs to Kendal. There are several car parks in the town – those by the river are the most convenient.

Getting there by train Kendal station is on a branch line. The nearest main line railway station is in Oxenholme, less than 3km (2 miles) away. Take the B6254 from Oxenholme to Kendal. Telephone (0345) 484950 for information.

From Kendal in the southern Lake District to Shap, Bampton and on to Pooley Bridge. From there the route takes in the entire length of Ullswater, follows Kirkstone Pass and returns to Kendal via single track and gated roads through the villages of Crook and Brigsteer.

Places of interest along the route

The views alone make this route special.

A Watchgate
The view from here towards Long Sleddale is splendid.

B Shap summit
A monument on Shap summit commemorates the importance of this pass to north–south communication, before the advent of the M6.

C Shap
At the top of a short climb, just outside Shap village, there are views to the right of Cross Fell and Great Dunn Fell and later, to the left, the dam at the head of Haweswater Reservoir and the surrounding fells.

D Aira Force
A convenient place for a break before tackling Kirkstone Pass. The views between Pooley Bridge and Aira Force, looking down over Ullswater, are especially rewarding. Aira Force is National Trust property. Café open April to November, daily. Waterfall accessible at all reasonable times. Admission free. Telephone (015394) 35599 for information.

E Kirkstone Pass
A close view of Red Screes and a distant view looking down to Lake Windermere.

F Helsington Barrows
A view of Kendal and the surrounding area from the west.

Lakeland view

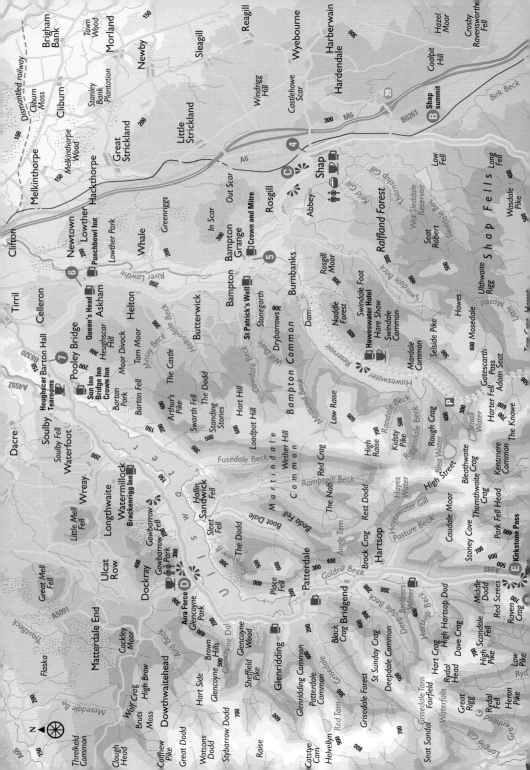

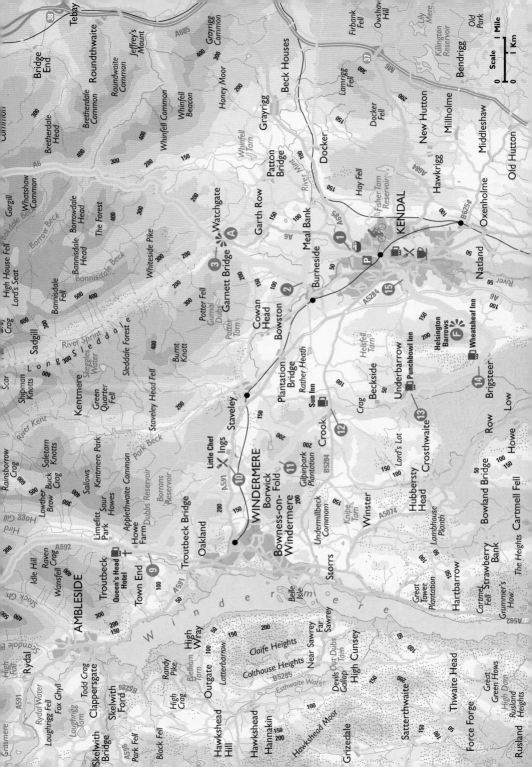

Route description

Leave Kendal on the A6 northwards towards Shap.

1 TL shortly after passing shopping complex on right, SP Shap Industrial Estate and Burneside. Follow road through estate following SP to Burneside.

2 TR just before Burneside (Burneside Hall on left), SP Long Sleddale, onto minor road (6.5km/4 miles). Continue on to Garnett Bridge.

3 For optional off-road route, TL at TJ, SP Long Sleddale and follow road running up Long Sleddale Valley. Approximately 7.5km (5 miles) along the valley, at Sadgill, the road divides into two tracks – take the track to the right of the stream and follow to Gatescarth Pass. Then descend to Haweswater car park. Continue along road on south side of Haweswater Reservoir to Burnbanks (shortly after Haweswater Hotel and dam) where RHF. Continue to Bampton and direction 5, where TL, SP Helton, Askham and Penrith.

Otherwise, TR at TJ, SP Shap and Kendal, Cycle up hill and TL at TJ onto A6 (11km/7 miles). Stay on A6 and cycle over Shap summit (21.5km/13.5 miles) and through Shap village.

4 TL onto minor road, SP Bampton, Haweswater and Shap Abbey (32km/20 miles). Pass track to Shap Abbey on left and continue to Bampton.

5 RHF after bridge, SP Helton, Askham and Penrith (39km/24 miles). Continue through Butterwick and Helton to Askham. Stay on road SP Penrith/Ullswater.

6 TL, on leaving Askham, onto single track road, SP Celleron. *45.5km (28.5 miles)*

7 TL at TJ onto B6320. Pass Barton Hall and cycle on to Pooley Bridge (52km/32.5 miles). Cross bridge. LHF after pier (A4592). Continue along Ullswater's west shore road, through Watermillock, Aira Force, Glenridding and Patterdale, past Brothers Water through Kirkstone Pass.

8 Descend towards Windermere, taking care on steep descent (74km/46 miles). Road starts to climb again, past Howe Farm.

9 TL onto minor road (opposite Troutbeck SP), and up hill. *81km (50.5 miles)*

10 TL onto A591 at Ings (care – busy road), and then immediately TR (after shelter on right), onto minor gated road (86.5km/53.5 miles). Follow this, under railway bridge and through a series of gates.

11 TL at Borwick Fold TJ (cattle grid), no SP, and on to Crook.

12 TL at TJ, onto B5284 (92.5km/57.5 miles). Then TR immediately after Sun Inn, SP Underbarrow. Continue past Beckside and into Underbarrow, where keep to road on left.

13 TR at TJ opposite Punchbowl Inn and immediately TL, SP Brigsteer. *97km (60.5 miles)*

14 Arrive Brigsteer. LHF by Wheatsheaf Inn, SP Kendal (100km/62 miles). Up long climb to Helsington Barrows, down hill, cross bridge over Kendal bypass and in to Kendal.

15 TR at Gillingate TJ in Kendal, down hill to Main Street where TL to join the one way system and return to the car park.

109.5km (68 miles)

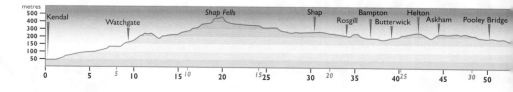

Ullswater

Food and drink

Shap has several pubs serving good bar meals and a grocers shop selling drinks, sandwiches and confectionery. Bampton Grange and Askham also have pubs serving bar meals, as do Pooley Bridge, Watermillock, Glenridding, Patterdale and Brothers Water. It is wise not to eat too much before tackling Kirkstone Pass. The Sun Inn, Crook,

Punchbowl Inn, Underbarrow and Wheatsheaf Inn, Brigsteer all serve bar meals.

Kirkstone Inn, Kirkstone
Excellent spot for refreshment before a long descent.

Queen's Head Hotel, Troutbeck
Bar meals available.

Little Chef, Ings
On the A591.

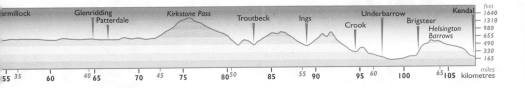

THE CTC

working for cycling

The CTC is Britain's largest national cycling organisation. Founded in 1878, the CTC has over 65,000 members and affiliates throughout the UK and overseas, and around 200 local groups. The CTC provides essential services for all leisure cyclists, whether you ride on- or off-road, and works to promote cycling and protect cyclists' interests.

CTC membership makes day-to-day cycling easier. A resident expert cycling engineer will answer all your technical queries about cycle buying, maintenance and equipment. And if you get ambitious about your cycling, the CTC's Touring Department has reams of information about cycling anywhere from Avon to Zimbabwe. There is also plenty of practical advice and information in the annual handbook. Then, when it comes to getting kitted out, the shop sells a wide variety of clothing, accessories, books, maps and guidebooks.

Cycling is good both for you and the environment; it is one of the healthiest activities there is, raising your metabolism, burning fat and toning muscle. However, accidents do happen, and the CTC's membership services mean that when you ride, you are protected by free third party liability of up to £1 million and by our legal assistance to pursue civil claims.

CTC members also receive *Cycle Touring and Campaigning* magazine free six times a year. *CT&C* takes pride in its journalistic independence. With reports on cycle trips all over the globe, forensic tests on bikes and equipment, and the most vigorous and effective pro-bike campaigning stance anywhere, *CT&C* is required reading for any cyclist.

It is not just members who benefit either: the CTC works on behalf of all Britain's 20 million cycle owners. Its effective campaigning at national level helped to create the Government's National Cycling Strategy. It is lobbying for lower speed limits on country lanes; campaigning so that you can carry bikes on trains; working with local authorities to make towns more cycle-friendly, to ensure that roads are designed to meet cyclists' needs and kept well maintained; making sure that bridleways are kept open; and negotiating cyclists' access to canal towpaths.

Whatever kind of cyclist you are: mountain biker, Sunday potterer, bicycle commuter, or out for the day with your family – cycling is easier and safer with the CTC's knowledge and services in your saddlebag. The CTC is the essential accessory for every cyclist!

For further information contact:
CTC
69 Meadrow
Godalming
Surrey
GU7 3HS

Telephone (01483) 417217
Fax (01483) 426994
e-mail: cycling@ctc.org.uk
Web: www.ctc.org.uk